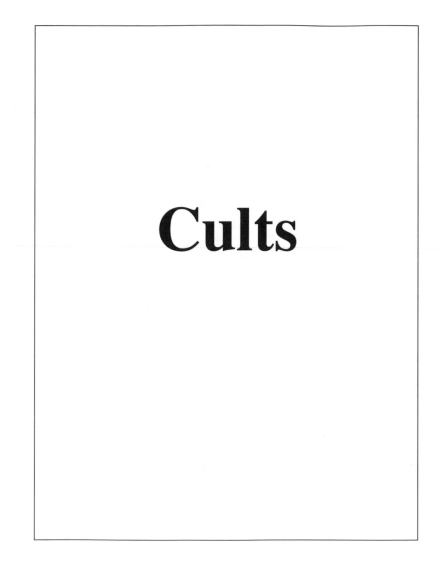

Cults

Look for these and other books in the Lucent Overview Series:

Cults

by Joan D. Barghusen

**LUCENT
BOOKS**

LUCENT *Overview Series*

LUCENT Overview Series

Library of Congress Cataloging-in-Publication Data

Barghusen, Joan D., 1935–
    Cults / by Joan D. Barghusen.
        p.   cm. — (Lucent overview series)
    Includes bibliographical references and index.
    Summary: Describes the nature and history of cults and the
different aspects of living in a cult, including the difficulty of
leaving it. *11-98   291.04609   (JU)*
    ISBN 1-56006-199–5 (alk. paper)
    1. Cults—United States—Juvenile literature.   2. United States—
Religion—1960—Juvenile literature.   [1. Cults.]   I. Title.
II. Series.
BP603.B36   1998
291'.046'0973—dc21   97–26652
                                                                             CIP
                                                                             AC

Copyright © 1998 by Lucent Books, Inc.
P.O. Box 289011, San Diego, CA 92198-9011
Printed in the U.S.A.

Contents

Introduction

CULTS HAVE BEEN a part of American society since the Pilgrims arrived in search of religious freedom. They offer alternatives to traditional religions that some people find more meaningful than the religions in which they were raised. Usually small and short-lived, most cults come and go without great public attention. Why then are cults controversial today?

First, the groups called cults are more numerous than they have ever been. Since the 1960s the United States has witnessed what has been called an explosion of cults. Some are related to Christianity; some are inspired by Eastern religions, such as Hinduism or Buddhism; and still others are not related to any known religion. Even their names present a bewildering array. Not all are limited to the United States, for cults exist worldwide and may be international in membership. At the same time, modern methods of communication, including worldwide computer networks, make these groups more visible than ever before.

Second, much controversy is generated when family conflicts over membership come to public attention. Sharp conflicts emerged in the 1970s and 1980s when many young adults between the ages of eighteen and twenty-five joined the new religions. Some parents who could not persuade their loved ones to leave the group became convinced that members were being held against their will. Fears of "brainwashing" and attempts to "deprogram," or change the beliefs and affiliations of cult members, continue to influence public opinion.

Controversy has been deepened by several recent tragedies involving the groups called cults. People struggle to understand the mass suicides of Heaven's Gate members in San Diego, California, the violent confrontation that destroyed the Branch Davidians of Waco, Texas, or the poison gas attacks in Tokyo subways by the Japanese cult Aum Shinrikyo. These tragic and violent events raise anxiety about cults in general.

A derogatory term

Adding to the controversy are the different opinions about what a cult is and what groups should be called cults. Once understood as a small group whose beliefs were outside the mainstream traditions of society, the term "cult" is now popularly used as a derogatory label. The stereotype of a cult portrays it as a destructive group that exploits its members and threatens their mental health. Once applied to a group, this stereotype purports to "explain" the group,

Members of the Hare Krishna religion, a sect of Hinduism, march in Washington, D.C. Many cults are offshoots of mainstream religions, and their number has proliferated in the United States since the 1960s.

even though little may be known about its beliefs or practices. Because of the derogatory way the term "cult" is now used, most researchers who study such groups no longer use the word, preferring the terms "alternative religions" or "new religious movements."

Cults are a fascinating topic to talk about, and people often express strong opinions about them. Yet most information that reaches the public about cults comes from media coverage of dramatic events or from anticult groups who warn about the dangers of so-called "destructive cults."

More balanced information about the wide variety of groups called cults is necessary in order to understand the cult controversy and to examine some of the questions it raises. Who joins a cult and why? What do cult members do? Why and how do they leave a group, and what happens when they do? Research studies and the reports of cult members themselves offer crucial information to help answer these questions and provide insight into the controversial topic of cults.

1

Definition and History

THERE IS MUCH confusion about the term "cult." Its basic meaning is simply the worship of a deity or the rituals of that worship. Historically it has been used to refer to unorthodox or unconventional groups whose beliefs are different from the traditional religions of the society in which they exist.

Because many people believe that their religion is the one true faith, they may call any other religion a cult, meaning the group holds mistaken or heretical beliefs. Thus the term is a subjective one. Often it is used in a derogatory way to demean the members of another group. In today's world, where no one religion dominates a culture and many religious traditions exist side by side in a country or a city, it is even less clear what groups should be called cults.

The use of the term as a derogatory stereotype increased through the 1970s as the anticult movement grew. According to J. Gordon Melton, director of the Institute for the Study of American Religion, this movement was made up primarily of parents who became disturbed by changes they saw in their children who joined certain religious groups. The negative perception of the term, fostered by activities of the anticult movement, has caused many researchers to abandon use of the word altogether. "It should be noted," Melton states, "that most writers, except for the harshest of anti-cult polemicists, have moved away from the term 'cult' and now use the less pejorative term 'new religion' to designate the more non-conventional religious groups in Western society."[1]

Margaret Thaler Singer, a clinical psychologist who has worked with thousands of current and former cult members and their families, has been active in the anticult movement. Recognizing that researchers do not agree on which groups should be identified as cults, she states that not all cults are religion-based groups. Instead, she says, a cult may form around one of many doctrines, theories, or practices. For example, she mentions consulting with members of a diet cult, a weight-lifting cult, and even a music camp cult. In defining a cult, Singer states that the term "denotes a group that forms around a person who claims he or she has a special mission or knowledge, which will be shared with those who turn over most of their decision-making to that self-appointed leader."[2] Singer is particularly concerned with groups she calls "destructive cults"; in these groups, she says, leaders use "thought reform," also called brainwashing, to manipulate and exploit members.

The different definitions used by experts confuse any discussion of cults. Adding to the confusion is the concept of thought reform, which Singer claims cults use to control

Though many cults, such as the Hare Krishna pictured here, are religious in nature, others may be based on secular ideas or lifestyles.

their members. In contrast, researchers David G. Bromley and Anson D. Shupe Jr. state emphatically, "There is no mysterious brainwashing process used to trap and enslave millions of young Americans."[3] They point out that groups of all types try to shape the attitudes of their members. To do this, a group may use methods of psychological persuasion or control. However, most researchers do not view these techniques as thought reform unless physical force or restraint is also used. Although most researchers do not accept the idea that cults use thought reform, still many have noted that the groups they studied used coercive psychological techniques to a greater or lesser degree.

The history of cults

Cults are not new. Such groups, which follow unconventional beliefs and practice in unusual ways, have consistently aroused suspicion and mistrust. Speaking of the present-day controversy surrounding cults, Elizabeth C. Nordbeck of Andover Newton Theological School points out, "Historically, new and unfamiliar religious movements (including Christianity itself) have emerged periodically and always have generated fear and antagonism disproportionate to their real threat."[4]

In its two hundred years of history, the United States has been home to many cults or alternative religions because of its guarantee of religious freedom. The first colonists, known as the Puritans or Pilgrims, were a group of reformers from the Church of England who were seeking a new home where they would be free to practice their religion. Another early group, seeking freedom of worship in the new world, was the English Shakers, who followed the teachings of Ann Lee, the group's religious leader who claimed to be the embodiment of Christ's female nature. Today, Nordbeck notes, this group no longer arouses the antagonism it once generated in society, and its few remaining members are generally regarded sympathetically by the American public. But she points out,

> In their heyday, however, the Shakers were as unconventional as any of today's new cults. Living in celibate communities

under the charismatic leadership of a female Messiah figure, they pursued a spartan, agrarian lifestyle, relieved only by the energetic rituals of dance and song from which they acquired their name.[5]

Cults of the nineteenth century

Many new cults emerged in the United States in the nineteenth century. The most successful was the Church of Jesus Christ of Latter-day Saints, popularly called the Mormons. Founded by Joseph Smith in 1830, its teachings and authority were based on visions Smith claimed to have received from angels and apostles of the Christian faith. The new group met with opposition from the very beginning, and it was forced to move from state to state. When Smith was murdered in Illinois, the group continued to move west, finding refuge at last in the Great Salt Lake Valley in Utah. Far from the major centers of population and power in the United States at the time, the new religion continued to grow in numbers. Today the Mormons claim millions of members in countries throughout the world and their beliefs have become accepted as an established religion.

Another cult of the nineteenth century was the Church of Christ, Scientist, popularly called the Christian Science Church. It was founded by Mary Baker Eddy, whose beliefs were based on the idea of unity with God. Since believers expect this state of unity to bring them health, members generally do not consult medical doctors. In spite of early opposition and ongoing controversy, Christian Science has found a place within the world's religions and has followers in many countries.

Other groups from the nineteenth century have not been as successful as the Mormons and the Christian Scientists. For example, Theosophists have persisted but remain relatively unknown. These occult groups formed

A lithograph of an early Mormon temple in Nauvoo, Illinois, which was built in 1841.

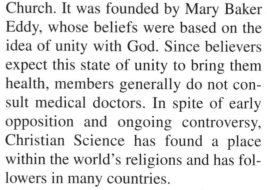

around the teachings of the Russian medium and psychic Helena Petrovna Blavatsky, who claimed to be able to contact the spirits of the dead. Today at least one hundred groups in North America have roots in the Theosophical movement. Other new religions from the nineteenth century have disappeared from history as their followers left, died, or sought other groups.

The Children of God

Many new cults emerged in the last few decades of the twentieth century. One of the earliest was the Children of God. A Christian-based group, it grew out of the Jesus People revival, a renewed interest in conservative Christianity among the youths of what has been called the counterculture movement. The term "counterculture" refers to the large numbers of disaffected young people of the 1960s who believed in "turning on" (seeking altered states of consciousness through drugs) and "tuning out" (ignoring the unsatisfactory world of society).

The Children of God was established as a ministry to young adults in Huntington Beach, California, by David Berg, later called Moses David, who was formerly a minister in the Christian and Missionary Alliance Church. After he allegedly received a vision that California would be struck by a major earthquake, Berg moved the group to Texas, where they lived communally and practiced sexual freedom. Berg viewed sex—which he equated with love— as a way for members to demonstrate God's love in the world. This group was the first of the new cults to spark organized opposition. Under pressure from angry parents of young members, the group moved its headquarters out of the United States. Known today as the Family of Love, the group exists quietly in small communes in several countries, including England and the Philippines.

Cults based on Eastern religious ideas

By the 1960s Eastern religious ideas had entered the West. Many Eastern practices were introduced to America by Asian immigrants who entered the country after 1965, when immigration laws became more hospitable to them. The new immigrants brought their religions and religious leaders, often called swamis, yogis, or gurus, with them.

The International Society for Krishna Consciousness was one of the first Eastern-oriented cults to achieve wide public attention in the United States. Popularly called the Hare Krishnas, members were often seen in airports and other public places, where they handed out literature. Their shaved heads and long yellow-brown robes made them noticeable as they sold flowers, asked for donations, or chanted their mantra, holy words that showed their devotion to Krishna:

Hare Krishna, Hare Krishna,
Krishna Krishna, Hare Hare
Hare Rama, Hare Rama
Rama Rama, Hare Hare.

Hare Krishna originated in India and was introduced to the United States by Swami Prabhupada. Members (pictured) believe that their devotion to Krishna will lead them to salvation.

Established hundreds of years ago in India, the worship of Krishna was brought to the United States by Swami Prabhupada, who is considered a Hindu saint. Hare Krishna converts believe that their loyalty to Krishna, an incarnation of the Hindu god Vishnu, will save them when the world ends. According to recent reports, this group shows signs of integrating into American society. According to Swami Chandra Mauli of a Chicago temple, "We have worked to create an environment where people can practice a spiritual life and also live within the world."[6]

Another cult based on Hinduism has not been so successful. In 1971 the Divine Light Mission was introduced into the United States by Guru Maharaj Ji, a thirteen-year-old boy from India. By 1978 it had several thousand members in a number of communes across the nation. Converts practiced daily meditation, an Eastern technique to attain spiritual enlightenment, as they sought to experience the divine light and other

Chanting and meditation as means toward spiritual enlightenment are integral parts of Eastern-influenced religious movements.

sensations associated with higher consciousness. However, many members became disillusioned when public events they held did not draw the large, enthusiastic crowds they anticipated. And when Maharaj Ji, who required celibacy of his followers, decided to marry, many members left. By 1984 the group had largely fallen apart.

Transcendental meditation

Groups based on Eastern traditions, such as the Hare Krishnas and the Divine Light Mission, all practice some form of chanting or meditation to achieve altered states of consciousness. By the 1970s the particular kind of meditation known as transcendental meditation had begun to spread rapidly throughout the United States. TM, as it was called, was introduced through centers established by the Hindu guru Maharishi Mahesh Yogi. The practice gained popularity, especially among young people, after it was adopted by the Beatles, the popular British rock group, and other celebrities.

In 1972 Maharishi announced his "World Plan," designed to bring enlightenment to the entire world through the practice of TM. For a while, TM was taught in some U.S. public schools and the armed forces until a court case declared that it was a religious practice and could not be supported by public funds. However, meditation in its various forms has become widely accepted in American society. Besides religious groups that use the technique to

The Reverend Sun Myung Moon, founder of the Unification Church.

attain spiritual enlightenment, therapeutic groups use meditation to reduce the stress of daily life, and some doctors prescribe it for health purposes.

The Unification Church

One of the best-known cults in America is the Unification Church of the Reverend Sun Myung Moon of Korea, whose converts are popularly called Moonies. Rev. Moon instituted his church in Korea in the late 1950s, expanded into Japan, and sent his first missionaries to the United States in 1959. Rev. Moon's ideas are outgrowths of Christianity, based on visions he claims instructed him to complete the unfinished mission of Jesus Christ. According to Moon's *Divine Principle*, Jesus failed to fulfill his mission because he did not marry and have children. Through the spiritual parenthood of Moon and his wife, the Unification Church seeks to establish the "Kingdom of God," bringing about world peace and the unity of nations. Like many other Christian cult leaders, Moon suggests that he is a messiah, and his followers think of him and his wife as "True Parents."

Magic and occult groups

Some recent groups have revived interest in the occult, such as the practices introduced in the nineteenth century by Madame Blavatsky. One of these is the Church Universal and Triumphant, founded by Mark L. Prophet in 1958. Its leaders are considered "Messengers of the Ascended Masters," spirits of those who have finished their cycle of lives on earth and attained wisdom, which they impart through the messengers. The most devoted members live communally at cult centers, where they train to become ministers of the faith.

A number of present-day cults practice magic, which members believe can effect change by invoking cosmic power. These groups are generally called neopagan, or new pagan, religions. Included among them are groups practicing witchcraft. Today most people who identify themselves as witches are followers of Wicca, a nature religion based on the worship of the Great Mother Goddess, who is called by different names, including Diana and Demeter. Some call Wicca the Old Religion, tracing it to the pre-Christian religion of Europe. In contrast to the popular misconception of witches as practitioners of black magic, the Wiccan ethical statement, "Lest ye harm none, do what you will," binds witches to do no harm. Besides Wicca, other neopagan cults include groups based on the traditions of ancient Norse, Druidic, or Egyptian gods.

Satanism

Traditional Satanism has a long history and is often confused with the recent Church of Satan, although the two have little in common. The writings of Anton LaVey, who founded the Church of Satan in the 1960s, advocate an indulgent lifestyle in which anything is permissible as long as it does not hurt someone else in an undeserved way. Illegal activities, and specifically animal sacrifices, are prohibited in the Church of Satan. This group has remained a small one, with membership estimated to be in the hundreds.

On the other hand, traditional Satanism, defined as the worship of the Christian devil, parodies and defiles the rites of Christianity, especially Catholicism. According to Melton's *Encyclopedic Handbook of Cults in America*, traditional Satanism has been inadvertently maintained by those who opposed it. Noting that the practice, though an old one, had produced almost no literature, he contends that "the maintenance of the tradition fell to non-Satanists, primarily conservative Christians, who authored many books thoroughly denouncing Satanism."[7] Melton claims that these writers described the practices of Satanism

Pagans celebrate the renewal of spring in New York's Central Park. Nature worship is common in neopagan religions like Wicca, which reveres the Great Mother Goddess.

in such great detail that today groups or individuals try to imitate what has been written. For the most part, those who practice this kind of Satanism are criminals, vandals, or delinquents who leave Satanic symbols at the scenes of their crimes.

More recently a new kind of Satanism has emerged in the reports of ritual Satanic abuse. Typically these charges are made by women in their thirties who claim to retrieve memories, while in counseling sessions, of sexual abuse that took place at the hands of Satanists when they were children. Sociologist Jeffrey Victor says little or no evidence exists to substantiate such claims and states, "Investigative journalists have proven some of these testimonials to be outright frauds."[8] Victor calls the widespread reports of Satanic ritual abuse "contemporary legends" similar to the stories that prompted the Salem witch trials, and he cautions that such legends have been used in the past to justify the persecution of unpopular groups, from religious dissenters to communists.

Santeria and religious freedom

Santeria is a religious group that practices animal sacrifice among its rituals. According to researcher Migene Gonzalez-Wippler, Santeria is a mix of Yoruba magical rites and traditions of the Catholic Church. It developed in Cuba when Africans of the Yoruba tribe, who were brought to the island as slaves, used the names of Catholic saints to try to disguise their traditional deities from Spanish overlords. Millions of people in Latin America practice this religion, and Cubans have brought it to parts of the United States, especially Florida.

The Santeria practice of sacrificing animals to provide blood offerings to the Yoruba saints has brought members of the group into conflict with neigh-

A Santeria follower in New York stands next to a sacrificial altar. Members of this group sacrifice animals to provide blood offerings to their deities.

bors and local authorities. In an effort to stop the sacrifices, the city council of Hialeah, Florida, passed four ordinances banning the ritual slaughter of animals, including pigs, chickens, and goats. Lawyers for Santeria responded by arguing that the ban was unfair. Since animals in Hialeah could be killed by hunting, trapping, and fishing, lawyers contended that it should be legal to kill them in a religious service. In 1993 the U.S. Supreme Court ruled unanimously that the city's ban on ritual animal sacrifice violated the religious freedom of followers of Santeria.

The issue of religious freedom surfaces often in relationship to groups considered cults in the United States. The fear and suspicion that surround these groups often lead to attempts to suppress them. But as theologian Harvey Cox states,

> The basic issue is still that of religious freedom. As bizarre as some of the new religious movements may seem to us (and some of them seem bizarre indeed), it is hard for people to see that oddness or distastefulness has nothing to do with a religious movement's claim to religious freedom. It is precisely *un*popular movements that most need due process of law, the supposition of innocence until proven otherwise, and the protection guaranteed by the Constitution.[9]

Cults exist in all the world's traditional religions

Cults are not limited to the United States, where the dominant religion is Christianity. They exist within all the world's major religions—Judaism, Islam, Hinduism, and Buddhism—and are found all over the world. Within the established belief systems, these small groups provide a place for believers who seek a different religious expression. Religious scholars say these unconventional religions can be a source of alternative religious ideas that can help large, conventional religions change and grow with the times. Such groups often seek to reform traditional religion by the changed beliefs or practices or to purify it by returning to earlier beliefs or practices.

Leading the reform movement in Buddhism is the group Nicheren Shoshu, which claims to be the "true" Buddhism.

Other alternative religions:

Poland: Zen Buddhism; Hinduism; Theosophy; Hawaiian Kahuna, a magic movement; Ordo Lux, a pagan occult movement; esoteric Yoga; Sikhism; Baha'i; Rastafarianism

Czech Republic & Slovakia: Buddhism; Baha'i; Unitarian Church

Hungary: Zoroastrianism; Unitarian Church

Slovenia, Croatia, Bosnia, Serbia, Montenegro, & Macedonia: The Theosophical Society; the Liberal Catholic Church, a mixture of Catholic and Theosophical thought; an initiatory magical order

Moscow: National UFO study centers; astrology study centers; the Russian Theosophical Society; national parapsychology schools

Romania: Unitarian Church

Bulgaria: The Religious Community of the "White Brethren," a spiritualistic brotherhood; The Children of God; Unitarian Church

Sources: Awake!, Back to Godhead, Inward Path, the Los Angeles Times, Religions Directory International. Map may not represent all unconventional religious groups.

Founded in Japan in the thirteenth century, Nicheren Shoshu has spread throughout the world in this century.

Within Islam there are many reform or fundamentalist groups that often use their interpretation of the Koran, the holy book of the Muslim faith, to validate social and political movements they favor. Some extremists among these groups have come to worldwide attention when they engaged in political or terrorist actions, such as the bombing of the World Trade Center in New York in 1993.

Cults and violence

Violent events involving cults have made headlines in the last two decades, beginning with the 1978 murders and suicides at the People's Temple in Jonestown, Guyana. The world was shocked when 912 men, women, and children at the jungle compound died by poisoning.

In 1993 the Branch Davidians of Waco, Texas, including many children, were killed during a fiery confrontation with the federal agents who were investigating the cult for firearms charges. And in 1994 more than fifty members of the Order of the Solar Temple died in simultaneous explosions, set off intentionally at their living quarters in Switzerland and Canada.

In Spring 1995 the world learned of deadly gas attacks in Tokyo subways, carried out by members of Aum Shinrikyo, a Japanese cult led by Shoko Asahara. More than a dozen people died and many were injured by the nerve gas sarin.

In March 1997 more cult deaths were reported as five more members of the Order of the Solar Temple killed themselves in Canada. Only a week later thirty-nine members of the UFO cult known as Heaven's Gate committed suicide to shed their "earthly containers," hoping to be transported by spaceship to a higher plane of existence.

Doomsday beliefs

Researchers say that groups with doomsday, or end-of-the-world, ideas are particularly prone to end in violence, perhaps because their belief in the imminent destruction of the world has prepared them for it. Such beliefs are common in Christian-oriented cults that are based on the New Testament Book of Revelation. But they also had a place in the beliefs of Aum Shinrikyo, a mix of Buddhist ideas and occultism, whose leader had predicted that Japan would be destroyed before the millennial year 2000. Imminent

Dead bodies litter the ground of the People's Temple in Guyana. Group members committed suicide in 1978 by drinking a mixture of Kool-Aid and cyanide.

Shoko Asahara (left), leader of Aum Shinrikyo, the cult responsible for the 1995 nerve gas attacks in the Tokyo subways.

destruction was also predicted by Heaven's Gate, whose members believed the earth would soon be "spaded over" and "recycled."

Number of cults and members

Since researchers disagree as to which groups should be called cults, facts and figures about the number of cults in existence are hard to gather. In addition, groups often form and dissolve quickly and may try to stay out of public view. Margaret Thaler Singer writes that three thousand to five thousand cults exist. Melton disputes these numbers and makes a more conservative estimate in his *Encyclopedic Handbook of Cults:* "Using the broad definition of the social scientists, one can find some 500 to 600 cults or alternative religions in the United States." [10]

It is even more difficult to assess the number of cult members. Not all groups make such figures available. Some groups may count anyone who has ever expressed an interest in their group, a practice that leads to greatly inflated numbers since the number who actually join the cult is much smaller. According to Melton's *Encyclopedic Handbook of Cults*, only about 10 percent of the people who attend an initial session ever become members of a cult. In contrast to Singer's statement that millions of people are involved in cults, Melton estimates that in 1992 there were approximately 150,000 to 200,000 active cult members in the United States.

2

Joining a Cult

ALL KINDS OF people join cults. They may be young or old, male or female, rich or poor, well-educated, or otherwise; and they may be of any race, ethnic origin, or previous religious affiliation. There are many different kinds of cults, or alternative religions, to receive them all.

But different cults do attract different kinds of people. For example, Santeria consists mostly of people from the ethnic groups among whom the practice originated. Jim Jones's People's Temple drew its members primarily from the urban poor in the inner-city neighborhood of San Francisco where Jones started his church. Members of the Branch Davidians came mostly from the Seventh-Day Adventist church, whose beliefs the Davidians wanted to reform.

Many of the new cults that originated in the 1960s and 1970s attracted mostly young people from the middle class. Often these young adults, who were just moving from their parents' homes to life on their own, left jobs or college educations to devote themselves to the cult. The entrance of this population of middle-class youth into cult experience brought cults into the public eye. The ensuing debate and controversies continue today.

According to Singer, many educated professionals have been attracted to recently developed groups that emphasize therapeutic techniques or the growth of self-awareness to transform the individual's personality. One of these groups is the Movement for Spiritual Inner Awareness (MSIA). Formed by John-Roger Hinkins in the early 1970s, the group seeks to transform the world by improving the individuals within it. The leader claims to have achieved total spiritual awareness, which others can learn through the programs of MSIA.

Today's well-known cults are often international in membership. For example, both the Unification Church and the Hare Krishnas have centers in over one hundred countries throughout the world. Any group that hopes to recruit new members may reach across national borders in its search for converts; even a small group may be international. The Branch Davidians, although a communal group of only about one hundred people, included members from at least four different countries.

People join cults for religious and idealistic reasons

Just as cults and their members are diverse, so are the reasons people join. Many give religious or idealistic reasons for joining a cult. They say they want to serve God, attain spiritual awareness, or live a more meaningful life. They may be drawn to the specific religious message of the group or the spiritual insights of the leader. One young woman who joined the Unification Church expressed her interest in its ideas, stating, "The questions the church was dealing with hadn't been in my Christian background. Questions about my purpose, my origin and God's charac-

Hare Krishnas march and chant in a Moscow park. The Hare Krishna movement has spread to over one hundred countries, including Russia, where it was introduced in 1980 and has flourished in recent years.

ter, things that I'd been asking for a long time, things I'd given up thinking about."[11] Some members of the Branch Davidians joined the cult because they were impressed by the leader's knowledge and interpretations of biblical scripture.

People who join cults for religious reasons may have been seeking spiritual enlightenment for some time, affiliating themselves with various groups before joining the cult. One young man, who had tried several groups and philosophies before he discovered the Unification Church, expressed his feeling of satisfaction after joining: "I had found my purpose in life. I now had conviction and belief, something which had been lacking before."[12]

Many members report being attracted by the goals of the group they joined. Commonly these goals include personal salvation and improving or saving the world. A veteran of the Vietnam War said he joined the Unification Church, whose stated goals include establishing world unity and bringing about peace, because he wanted to help end war.

People join cults for social and personal reasons

Many people join cults because the group makes them feel good. They report feeling completely accepted by group members in a way they had never found in the outside world. A member of the Hare Krishnas reported that he joined for the security and friendship cult members offered. Researcher Eileen Barker states that some of the Unification Church members she studied joined the group because they were attracted to the loving community they found there.

Some people join cults because their friends or family are members, perhaps a boyfriend or girlfriend, or a brother or sister. Young children become members without any choice on their part, entering cults in the care of their parents, or being born into the group. Other people simply like the idea of living in a commune and do not care greatly about the underlying philosophy of the group as long as they feel comfortable. While many consider the

Hare Krishna boys and girls pose for a photograph. Young children are brought into cults when their parents join or when they are born to parents who are already members.

move carefully, some report joining a cult because they had nothing else to do or because they found it easier to join than to resist the recruiters. Some members even said they joined because they felt sexually attracted to the person who recruited them.

People also report joining cults because they hope the group will help them deal with a specific personal problem. For example, one man joined the Unification Church because he thought its requirement of celibacy for unmarried members would help him avoid problems he had encountered in his relationships with women. Likewise, people who have used drugs to achieve altered states of consciousness often join cults that practice meditation or other techniques promising altered states without the necessity of drugs.

Therapy cults and groups designed to promote self-awareness appeal to people who are seeking psychological and spiritual growth through the group. These members may be in search of an answer to a specific problem or need. Singer identifies many of the groups they join as cults, based on her claim that the leaders use thought reform to control and exploit members. These groups may be large and formally organized or they may be small, informal, and nonreligious in their activities. Singer mentions, as examples, a self-improvement group, which emphasized dieting, and a "prosperity" cult, which promised members would learn to "gather" money, love, and power.

Some people who feel dissatisfied with life in general, or disillusioned with the world, may be attracted to groups that withdraw from society, keeping to themselves in order to live more "pure" lives. A member of the Heaven's Gate cult, who left the group a month before the suicides, expressed the lack of meaning he found in life to a *Newsweek* interviewer, saying that he had had nothing at the time he first heard the group's ideas. Intrigued by its belief that souls could leave the earth to advance to a stage beyond human existence, he convinced cult members to let him join.

Are people who join psychologically troubled?

Based on her work with former cult members, Margaret Thaler Singer finds that there is not a particular type of person who joins a cult; rather it is someone in a particular set of circumstances. Explaining her conclusion, Singer says, "I have found that two conditions make an individual especially vulnerable to cult recruiting: being depressed and being in between important affiliations."[13]

Researchers do not agree on whether people who join cults are apt to be depressed or psychologically troubled in some way. Psychiatrist Marc Galanter found that 30 percent of the members of a Unification Church group that he studied in the United States reported seeking professional help, such as counseling, for serious emotional problems before they joined. On the other hand, Eileen Barker, who studied members of the Unification Church in London, and Wolfgang Kuner, a German researcher, have not found evidence to support the idea that those who join cults are more psychologically troubled than other people of the same age and sex.

Many researchers, however, agree that those who join cults are likely to be without current affiliations or attachments. They may be away from home and friends, or perhaps they have just lost a job, broken off a relationship, lost a loved one through death, or left school or church. It is at in-between stages such as these, the researchers say, that a person is apt to be open to new ideas and groups. Galanter's study of Unification Church members supported this idea when he found that those who considered joining the church but finally chose not to showed more outside affiliations than those who actually joined.

Transitions

Lack of affiliations or connections with family and friends, school, church, or work, most often occurs when a person is in a state of transition, or change. Several researchers have pointed out that the transition from adolescence to adulthood plays an important part in the tendency of young people to join cults. The situation a young person faces at this stage of life—the separation from home and family, the desire for new relationships, the necessity to choose a career or direction in life, and the need to become self-supporting—may make cults, with their set agendas and built-in communities, seem an attractive course to take.

The statements of one young man who was a member of the Unification Church for four and a half years revealed that joining the cult solved many problems for him. He said he felt that a burden had been lifted from him when he made the decision to join: "Now I had a place to sleep and eat. Friends. I had a belief and there was work to do."[14]

But transitions do not only occur in young adulthood. Another important transition occurs as adults grow into the elderly stage of their lives. And, as Singer points out, the elderly are also attracted in increasing numbers to cults, including some that appeal to the desire for eternal life. To reach more potential members among the older generation, Singer says that "some cults have cen-

The sense of community and purpose that cults offer fills a void in the lives of young people searching for direction and personal connection. Here, a young follower of an Indian guru meditates.

A Hare Krishna stands next to a display designed to discourage meat eating. Hare Krishnas are publicly active and often distribute literature to spread their messages.

tered their recruitment drives in states like Arizona and Florida, where many elderly retire."[15]

Recruitment

Recruitment, or the process of bringing in new members, varies by cult, but almost always happens step-by-step. It begins with an initial expression of interest and ends when the new member makes a commitment to the group. Recruitment often consists of informal conversations with cult members or visits to the cult center. Large groups may have more formal programs, including lectures and seminars. Some groups, such as witches and neopagans, do not actively recruit at all, and those who are interested must seek out groups on their own.

Most of the research on cults since the 1960s has focused on middle-class youths and the groups they join. Among the large groups whose recruiting programs have been studied are the Unification Church and the Hare Krishnas. Both groups offer a series of events that are planned to attract, interest, and inform prospective members.

While groups may advertise on bulletin boards or in newspapers, most often the process of recruitment begins with a personal contact. The cult recruiter looks for a likely prospect to approach; typically, this is someone who is alone, especially someone who appears lonely or new to the area. The recruitment can take place on the street, in a park, at a bus station, or at some other public place. The recruiter introduces himself and tries to engage the potential member in friendly conversation, perhaps asking the person's name and where he or she is from, or making other small talk. Or, the recruiter may have literature, flowers, or candy to sell as an introduction. When a prospect seems interested, the recruiter will invite him or her to dinner or a meeting at the group center.

At this first meeting, the potential member will be showered with attention and interest, even affection, and made to feel very welcome and comfortable. Usually there will be a lecture, a film, or some other presentation to give the visitor an introduction to the group. There may also be dinner and singing or other entertainment. If the person continues to show interest, he or she will be invited to a more in-depth activity, perhaps a weekend seminar. The next step will be a more intense set of workshops, in some cases lasting for several weeks. By this time, the potential member will probably be asked to make a commitment to the group.

A member of the Unification Church teaches passers-by about the principles of his group.

If the person decides to join, there may be a period of probation for three to six months, after which both member and group make the final decision about full membership. Thus, joining is a gradual process from the first contact to the full acceptance of the member into the group.

Deceptive techniques

Many complaints by anticultists center on deceptive practices in recruitment. They charge that prospective members are not told the nature of the group until they have already formed relationships with cult members and feel committed to the group. They say that people are lured into joining by this deception and the excessive attention lavished on them during recruitment. They point out that some cult members themselves call the deceit "heavenly deception" and think it is justified by the good of their cause.

But most researchers who have studied cults, or even gone through the process of recruitment themselves, generally found that deception was not a common practice. Most recruiters, they say, identified themselves as members of their group at the first contact. Furthermore, there were usually pictures of the cult leader and information about the cult and its goals prominently displayed at the center where meetings were held.

Although sociologist Thomas Robbins cites that many researchers have acknowledged that some groups use deceptive and coercive pressures, Melton maintains that most of the serious charges of deceptive practices can be traced to a couple of cult groups in California in the 1970s, and he believes the practice has since died out. He also points out that the distinctive dress of some cult members, such as the Hare Krishnas, would make it difficult for them to be deceptive. And he notes that at least one recent group has its prospective members fill out a form to acknowledge that they are aware that they are about to participate in an event sponsored by the group. "While new members may not be aware of all of the implications of joining a distinctively different religion," Melton concludes, "they do understand

"Fred, do you want to join a cult?"

the basic beliefs and requirements and the identity of the group they are joining."[16]

Still Singer claims that, in her experience of counseling people who have left cults,

> Former cult members commonly reveal that they were looking for companionship or the chance to do something to benefit themselves and mankind. They say they were not looking for the particular cult they joined and were not intending to belong for a lifetime. Rather, they were actively and/or deceptively pressured to join, soon found themselves enmeshed in the group, were slowly cut off from their pasts and their families, and became totally dependent on the group.[17]

Singer contends that cults use thought reform, which she says is a coordinated program of persuasion of which the recruit is unaware. She says cults use thought reform to change people, making them dependent on the group so they will put its goals ahead of their own well-being.

Other researchers reject the claims of thought reform, asserting that, if thought reform is at work and is as dangerous as anticultists claim, cults would be more effective at recruitment than they are.

How many people join?

Research shows that even among those people who are curious enough to go to a group's initial meeting, only a small proportion return for another visit. A study in the United States by Galanter found that only 6 percent of an original group of 104 recruits who took a two-day workshop in the Unification Church were still with the church four months later. This proportion is similar to the numbers reported by Eileen Barker for a group of Unification Church recruits in London.

Melton, too, states that more than 90 percent of those who join an alternative religion leave it within a few years. Even the well-known contemporary cults, such as the Unification Church and the Hare Krishnas, have only a few thousand members, he says, pointing out, "Most cults have only a few hundred members and spend most of their energy just surviving."[18]

3

Life in a Cult

ONCE RECRUITED, THE new cult member begins to learn more about the group's mission and to work toward its goals. If the group lives together, the new member will move into a group center. This center may be an apartment or house in a city or town, or a farm or rural compound.

While every cult is different, some aspects of communal cult life are similar. First of all, members' activities are highly structured, or planned for them. The needs of the cult and instructions of cult leaders dictate what is to be done. Members are expected to carry out the plans and programs, and most have little or no role in decision making. Secondly, members spend most, if not all, of their time with each other. The demands of cult membership are often so time-consuming that members give up school or jobs and abandon relationships with family and noncult friends.

Closeness of the group is supportive

Cult members are seldom alone. At the commune or living center, they are part of a group. They eat, work, study the principles of the group, and even socialize almost exclusively with each other. If sent out to recruit, they usually go in teams of two or more. Through this constant association, members typically come to rely on each other for affection and emotional support.

Many cult members praise the loving, supportive atmosphere of the group and the sense of belonging they felt when they joined it. As one woman recalls, "I had the expe-

Hare Krishnas dance and chant to raise money for their sect. The communal aspect of cult life extends beyond the cult center itself: Those who work and recruit outside the cult community do so in groups.

rience of feeling more loved and accepted than I'd ever felt in my whole life."[19] This closeness and belonging provides strong support for members, especially when they must defend their faith against questions or ridicule by outsiders.

Closeness of group helps control behavior

However, the close group, with its strong emotional ties, is not just supportive. It is also a powerful force for controlling behavior since it sets up an expectation that people will conform to its ideas and actions. Members who do not conform risk losing the group's approval.

Members who do not go along with leaders or programs may be reprimanded, ostracized, or punished in an attempt to bring their behavior into line. While this might be a gentle correction offered in a loving way, it can also be a harsh physical punishment or an unkind rejection. One group disciplined uncooperative members by putting them "in quarantine." While they were not physically restrained, other group members, including their own family members, were not permitted to speak or have any contact with them.

Likewise, members are often discouraged from expressing any questions or doubts they have about the group or its ideas; and they themselves may feel it is disloyal to doubt. One member of the People's Temple reported putting aside her misgivings because she thought it was disruptive to the group's mission to criticize the leader, even when she doubted his methods. Other cult members report simply having no time for doubt, since they are kept busy with planned activities that leave no occasion for free discussion.

Worship or study of beliefs

Typically, cult members spend a part of each day in devotions, prayer, meditation, or study of the principles of the cult. These activities take widely different forms, depending on the group. In a Hare Krishna temple, activities are strictly scheduled around the rituals for worship. Followers arise before dawn each day to pray, chant, and make food offerings to the deity at regular times throughout the day. Before and after the rituals, there are lectures or study time when devotees study the sacred writings of Krishna or participate in other activities, which might include public chanting of the Hare Krishna mantra.

While most cults do not have such regimental rituals as the Hare Krishnas, many Christian-based cults have long hours of sermons, prayer, or Bible study. If the group does

Worship in a Hare Krishna temple includes prayer, chanting, offerings of food, and studying.

An Aum Shinrikyo member sits in front of photos of leader Shoko Asahara and a list of ten commandments to guide followers' behavior.

not use rituals or scriptures from established, traditional religions, it may rely on writings, audiotapes, or video messages furnished by the leader to provide materials to guide the study and thinking of members.

Although a small, informal cult may lack written statements of belief, the leader spends time transmitting his worldview or demonstrating his special powers to members. In the Manson Family cult, leader Charles Manson conveyed his ideas through songs and stories. Acting out the wishes of the leader, members of this group murdered actress Sharon Tate, her friends, and others in the Los Angeles area in August 1969. Manson hoped the brutal murders and the slogans cult members left scrawled in blood, would provoke social chaos, bring about world conflict, and install him as the leader of the survivors. He had promised to lead his followers to an underground paradise in the desert to keep them safe during the time of chaos. According to Vincent Bugliosi, the attorney who prosecuted Charles Manson for his part in the murders, "The Family loved to hear Charlie sermonize about this hidden 'land of milk and honey.'"[20]

Witnessing

In some cults members may be sent out to "witness," or tell others about their faith. Usually witnessing is done in teams, with two or more members circulating in a public place or going house-to-house in a neighborhood. The public displays of chanting and dancing by Hare Krishnas is a form of witnessing. Devotees call the ritual *sankirtana* and consider it an act of devotion to the god.

Witnessing may coincide with fund-raising as members ask for donations in return for literature or sell flowers, candy, peanuts, or other small items. Often new recruits are assigned to these activities, which cult members say can help to strengthen their will. Some report that the rejection and ridicule they often face helps to reinforce their feeling of separation from the outside world, binding them to the cult. As authors Carroll Stoner and Jo Anne Parke state, "The fund raising of the Moonies and the Krishnas not only deepens their sense of mission but also widens the gap between them and the world they have left behind."[21]

A couple in an airport gives money to a Hare Krishna after accepting a book from him. Soliciting funds from a sometimes harsh public reinforces the rift between cult members and the outside world.

Work for the goals of the group

Since members furnish the workforce that carries out the group's mission, they may do any kind of work the cult undertakes. They may be part of an international business run by a large group, such as the Unification Church, or they may work on one of the farms or in one of the restaurants of the Hare Krishnas. They may write newsletters or arrange lectures and travel schedules for cult leaders. Or, they may perform housekeeping tasks, such as cooking or cleaning for the group.

Even if a task is unpleasant or the work violates a member's ethical standards, cult members are expected to do it for the sake of the cause. Typically, the goals of the group are seen as so important that they justify whatever means are taken to achieve them. In extreme cases, members may carry out violent or illegal acts, such as the Manson Family murders or the Aum

Shinrikyo gas bombings, to fulfill the wishes of the leader or further the ends of the group.

Standard of living

Life in a cult commune is usually simple and often spartan. Most groups cannot afford or do not encourage luxuries. Only the most basic living accommodations are provided, often with crowded dormitory-type sleeping quarters, giving little privacy. Sometimes members sleep in sleeping bags on the floor. The cult's few possessions, which might include a television or a car, are shared. In some groups members even share clothing so that an individual has no personal possessions at all.

While a few groups may prosper, Melton points out that most groups struggle to survive financially. Even though members share whatever possessions or wealth they have and are often encouraged to ask their families for money, the lifestyle for most cults remains poor. Sometimes members work at regular jobs and donate their salaries to the group. Members of Heaven's Gate designed computer websites to support their group. In spite of critics' claims that Unification Church fund-raisers collect millions of dollars, members of a fund-raising team in Boston claimed only to be supporting themselves. According to Stoner and Parke, who accompanied the team one day, "They only fund-raise to keep their individual centers going, they say." [22] The authors note that this particular team had raised thirty dollars in the morning and less in the afternoon.

The tasks of daily life, such as shopping for food, preparing meals, and cleaning up may be shared among members, or they may be assigned to particular people. The quality of food depends on who does the cooking. Meals are usually simple and, in some groups, vegetarian. If funds are adequate, meals can be nourishing, and communes that have gardens may provide especially healthy eating. One mother said that her two daughters had blossomed while living on a farm commune. More common, however, are the complaints of family members who charge that their loved one in a cult suffers from malnutrition

Hare Krishna devotees raise funds in New York. Cult incomes usually come from donations and the salaries of members who hold jobs outside the group.

because of the poor food provided or because intensive work schedules interfere with regular meals.

Housing is likely to be in a run-down property in a poor neighborhood. One mother found the condition of the building that housed her son's Hare Krishna temple so deplorable that she reported it to the local fire officials. The People's Temple commune at Jonestown, Guyana, was under investigation for substandard living conditions when it met its tragic end.

It is not uncommon for cult members to neglect their own physical well-being out of enthusiasm for the cause. Researchers found that traveling teams of fund-raisers for one group slept in their unheated van rather than use part of the money they had raised to stay in a motel. In many cults, self-sacrifice is encouraged by a sense of urgency about the group's mission and by the group's idea that materialism and luxury are sinful. To encourage unselfishness, children in the People's Temple were given allowances but then instructed to donate them back to the group. Those who did not give up their money were punished.

Sex and marriage

Most cults regulate the sexual practices of their members in some way. Some require members to be celibate, refraining from all sexual relationships. In both the Unification Church and the Hare Krishnas, sexual relations are permitted only for married couples and then only for the purpose of creating children. Unification Church members are not allowed to marry without the permission of leaders, who choose marriage partners for them.

At the opposite extreme, the Family of Love encourages free sex among its members. At one time, leader Moses David also urged young female members to use sex as a way to attract men to the cult. However, strong interpersonal attachments that might interfere with loyalty to the group were discouraged. In some cults, the male leader claims sexual rights to all the women in the group. This was the case in the Manson Family, where the leader taught that nothing was immoral or wrong; whatever happened was right. The leader may also claim the right to multiple marriages, as was the case with David Koresh of the Branch Davidians, who then prohibited all other sexual relations in the group.

If a marriage relationship interferes with dedication to the cult, the group may try to come between the spouses or use one of them to put pressure on the other to follow cult routines or instructions. Some cults assign husbands and wives to different communes, interrupting their lives together. Loyalty to the cult is seen as a higher priority than dedication to the marriage.

Roles of men and women

In many cults men are favored for positions of leadership and responsibility, while women are assigned to subordinate, or supporting, roles. This is especially common in fundamentalist, or Bible-based, cults where women are seen as subservient to men, as they were in the society of the biblical patriarchs.

Researcher Francine Jeanne Daner also saw this attitude among the Hare Krishnas she studied. "Ideally," she explains, "the woman must be completely submissive and a constant servant to her husband."[23] This expectation for the woman's behavior becomes a constant source of friction, making marriages within the Hare Krishnas difficult.

A man who housed the Manson Family for a few months reported to prosecuting attorneys that he and Charles Manson would talk and sing songs while the women did the housekeeping and cooking and tended to the men's needs. When asked about Manson's attitude toward women, another informant responded, "Women had only two purposes in life, Charlie would say: to serve men and to give birth to children."[24]

In other cults, women may have leadership roles and gender is not an important factor in the assignment of duties. Group leaders are sometimes women, such as Clare Prophet of the Church Universal and Triumphant. And some groups, including witches, are made up primarily of women.

Lives of children

Children in cults share the living conditions and experiences of their parents. However, parents may not be as important as the cult family. Children may even be separated from their parents at an early age to be cared for by various cult members, so they will learn to think of the group as their family. Often cult members make up the only family children know, since contacts with grandparents or other relatives outside the cult may be strongly discouraged.

Women in the Manson Family (pictured) were expected to serve the male members and bear children.

In groups with a strong authoritarian leader, children may be instructed to call the cult leader "father." According to reports of medical personnel and social workers who interviewed the children of Branch Davidians released during the standoff with federal agents, the children spoke of leader David Koresh as both their father and as God. And when asked to draw pictures of their family, the children did not draw their mothers and fathers but drew pictures of adult cult members.

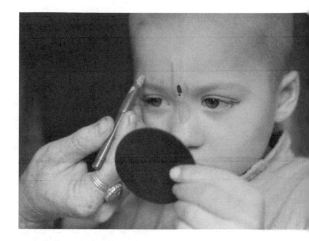

A Hare Krishna child, such as this one, is left undisciplined until age five, when he or she begins attending school and is expected to adhere to stricter rules of conduct.

In many groups, discipline is strict and punishments harsh, even for young children. This is especially true in fundamentalist cults, since these adults believe children must be punished because they are born in a state of sin. Child-rearing ideas are different for the Hare Krishnas, who instruct parents to let children do as they please for the first five years of life. During this time they are cared for primarily by their mothers. At age five, children go to school and are expected to learn discipline, which becomes ever stricter as they grow older.

Children's education

At an early age children usually begin attending lectures, study groups, and worship sessions to learn the ideas of the group. Although some cults send their children to public schools, groups who want to shelter children from the world may give them lessons inside the commune, as the Branch Davidians did, or set up their own schools. The school of the Divine Light Mission, briefly maintained in Denver, Colorado, even admitted noncult members.

Children who live in cults are isolated from the world in many ways. Often they have been taught to be fearful of the "evil" or "impure" outside world. Sometimes they are kept from even basic medical care, either by poverty or by a belief that faith will heal them. A few children may occasionally be allowed to visit a family member outside the cult, but for most kids, school is the only outside contact they are likely to have. And, even if they go to school, their knowledge and expectations of the world are limited and strongly affected by the cult's viewpoint.

Conversion

Those who join cults are said to have been "converted." Conversion implies that a change has occurred in the person's thinking or worldview that allows him or her to accept the group's beliefs and share its practices. Conversion also implies that the member has become committed to the group. Exactly how and when conversion happens is a subject of debate. Some cult members report experiencing a moment of truth when they became convinced that the group's beliefs were right. But for most, conversion is a gradual process that occurs over time.

Anticultists claim that conversion results from the thought reform processes cults use in recruiting and holding members. However, most researchers reject this idea, believing it is too extreme to describe the methods used. Researcher Robert Balch, who studied the Bo and Peep cult, an earlier version of Heaven's Gate, describes the typical process of conversion:

> The first step in conversion to cults is learning to *act* like a convert by outwardly conforming to a narrowly prescribed set of role expectations. Genuine conviction develops later beneath a facade of total commitment, and it fluctuates widely during the course of a typical member's career. Many cult believers never become true believers, but their questioning may be effectively hidden from everyone but their closest associates."[25]

As Balch's statement indicates, some cult members simply go along with the group, or they join with an experimental attitude while reserving judgment about converting. And those who do convert, say researchers, do so for different reasons. Some people come to an intellectual acceptance of the group's worldview, and some are converted by ties of affection they feel for the group. Whatever the basis of their conversions, those who stay with a group generally move to new levels of commitment over time.

4

Cult Organization

ACCORDING TO SOCIOLOGISTS William S. Bainbridge and Rodney Stark, a cult develops when a leader who claims to have special spiritual knowledge or abilities, or a special role in the universe, transmits his or her ideas to others who accept them. "We conceptualize successful cult innovation," state Bainbridge and Stark, "as a social process in which innovators both invent new religious ideas and transmit them to other persons in exchange for rewards."[26] Some rewards may be intangible, such as giving attention to the leader, accepting his or her beliefs, or participating in group activities; but they may also include rewards of money, property, or other valuables given by cult members.

It is not only the leader who is rewarded when a cult develops. Cult members hope to share in the leader's knowledge, abilities, or position by becoming followers. Being part of the cult's special mission gives them a sense of importance. The group's agenda provides activities, other members provide emotional support, and in many cases the group offers a home.

Family organization

Many cults adopt the pattern of the traditional nuclear family. Leaders are viewed as spiritual parents and are called "father" or "mother." Followers may be called "brothers" and "sisters," titles that reflect their subordinate relationship to the leaders and their peer relationship with each other in the hierarchy of the family.

David Koresh, leader of the Branch Davidians, believed he was the messiah.

Many Bible-based groups are organized on the model of the family, with the leader assuming the role of a powerful patriarch, like the clan leaders known from biblical scripture. When a patriarchal leader claims to be a messiah, as David Koresh of the Branch Davidians did, he is able to exert more control over group members' lives. For example, Koresh took several wives in order to father a new House of David, the line of biblical kings that gave rise to Jesus. In his role as supreme authority, Koresh held the trust and loyalty of his followers. Most of them died with him in April 1993 during the standoff with federal officials and the subsequent fire in their compound.

Monastic groups

Some cults organize themselves as monastic groups, like monks and nuns in more traditional religions. As in a family, leaders of monastic orders are called "father" or "mother," and the devotees "brother" and "sister." Monastic communities are almost always celibate; members believe that refraining from sexual relations allows them to be more fully devoted to the practice of their religion.

The group called Heaven's Gate, which came to national attention when its members committed suicide in March 1997, patterned itself on monastic life. They called the rented mansion in which they lived their temple and introduced each other as sister or brother. The group was celibate and kept themselves apart from society, except for necessary contacts in the business of designing computer websites, by which they supported themselves.

Leaders and followers

Most cults have a single strong leader who is charismatic, or exhibits the power to attract and hold followers. In the closed group of a cult, where members are isolated from the outside world, the power of an authoritarian leader may grow unchecked. The leader's self-image may grow ever more grandiose as he or she is bolstered by the support and adoration of cult members.

While the group's acceptance of the leader and his or her beliefs is sometimes thought to be a result of mind control, Charles Manson explained his control of followers in a more ordinary fashion, stating in court that "you can convince anybody of anything if you just push it at them all the time. They may not believe it 100 percent, but they will still draw opinions from it, especially if they have no other information to draw their opinions from." [27]

From the follower's point of view, Scott Lowe, now a professor of religious studies at the University of North Dakota, reflects on his experience as a young man in a cult:

> The bottom line is that I feel that most of the socialization I experienced was the product of my own will and desires; Da Free John [the leader of the group he joined] was a splendid salesman, to be sure, convincing hundreds of us that he was the only true master of our time and the only route to liberation, but we coaxed, enticed, and cajoled ourselves and each other into accepting his claims. We are responsible for that choice; no irresistible outside force ran off with our intellects." [28]

Charles Manson commanded a powerful hold over his followers, even influencing some of them to commit murders in 1969.

Just as members of a group may adopt a similar outward appearance, they also cultivate similarities of thought. Since group will is often mistaken by outsiders for a sign that the cult leader has brainwashed or imposed his will on followers, Heaven's Gate members left videotaped messages stating that their decision to commit suicide was made of their own volition. The leader then explained the group's belief that the earth was about to be destroyed and that salvation lay only in leaving earth by way of a spaceship. Seeing the appearance of the Hale-Bopp comet as a sign that the spaceship had come, all thirty-nine members of the cult, including the leader, committed suicide so their spirits could journey to heaven.

Secondary leaders

In groups that live communally, such as the Manson Family, the Branch Davidians, and Heaven's Gate, the

Heaven's Gate cult was lead by Marshall Applewhite, shown here in a video used for recruiting. Applewhite committed suicide with thirty-eight other members of Heaven's Gate in 1997.

leader can govern and communicate ideas by personal contact. Even a rather large group, such as the People's Temple, which had grown to almost 1,000 members when it moved to its commune in the jungle of Guyana, can rely on personal contact with the leader as long as the group lives together. While Rev. Jones relied on trusted helpers to manage the group's resources, discipline or punish members, and protect the group from outsiders, he himself retained all authority. Through personal appearances in long meetings and sermons, he continued to dominate the group, finally ordering the murders and suicides that killed 912 members by poison.

However, in large cults with many group centers, members may have little or no personal contact with the cult leader, who must rely on secondary leaders to carry out the work of the group. As in any organization, those who hold positions of authority have usually been with the group long enough to show that they understand its mission and goals and that they can be trusted to carry out the leader's orders. But structures are informal and helpers are usually chosen from among the leader's favorites, or from members who force themselves to attention. One young member of the Unification Church reported how he won the position of bus commander for the state, an important job in which he was responsible for a mobile bus team that roamed the state to get people interested in coming to church centers for lectures and workshops: "I got the job the same way nearly all jobs were gotten there: I showed I wanted it, I pushed and hustled and maneuvered."[29]

Linking leaders and members

Some groups have a series of steps or initiations through which members advance in insight or practice. Devotees of Hare Krishna or practitioners of Santeria must have their achievements noted or certified by a member of higher standing before they can move to the next level of proficiency. Thus the authority of lower-level leaders or initiates is passed down from higher authorities of the group.

In groups with scattered sites, the danger of splitting apart increases as local leaders become proficient and powerful. This happened to the Hare Krishnas, who have split into two different sections with separate leadership.

To avoid group division and keep members motivated and enthusiastic, large cults must find ways to keep the supreme leader present in the minds of members. The leader may appear at occasional lectures or events, such as the mass weddings performed by Rev. Moon. All of the methods of modern communication, from letters and telephone calls to videotapes and e-mail, are used to link leaders and members. Cyberspace websites also provide an outlet for leaders to communicate directly to large numbers of people besides their members.

Lay members and noncommunal groups

Cults with communal living groups may also have lay members, who live apart from the group and have a looser connection with it. For example, besides the devotees who live in temples and keep a demanding schedule of worship, the Hare Krishnas have lay members who live in their own homes, come to the temple for rituals once a week or so,

The Reverend Sun Myung Moon of the Unification Church presides over a 1982 mass wedding that included over two thousand couples.

and help support the temple with donations. Lay members can help a group build membership and integrate itself into the larger society, a necessity if it is to survive and grow.

Some groups are largely noncommunal, such as Nicheren Shoshu of America. Based on the teachings of a thirteenth century Buddhist monk, Nicheren Shoshu came to the United States in the 1950s. Its goal is to bring happiness and peace to the world by teaching its principles to as many people as possible. Instead of communal living groups, this group relies on its many organizations, such as children's groups and young adult groups, to build solidarity and form the close-knit group necessary to support the cause.

Many noncommunal groups do not have the strong leader seen in cults where members live together. But because their beliefs diverge so much from the norms of mainstream society, they are often called cults. Among these groups are the so-called therapy cults that have de-

veloped over the past few decades, promising members psychological well-being or personal growth through their systems of analysis and training.

Therapy groups

The best known of the therapy groups is the Church of Scientology. Originally called Dianetics, this therapeutic system was developed by science-fiction writer L. Ron Hubbard. He claimed it would erase bad patterns and memories from the past to make members "clear" of obstacles that retarded their happiness and effective functioning. Over time, Hubbard added his theory that human beings were originally celestial entities called thetans, who became trapped in the earthly dimension. His therapeutic techniques are designed to help members return to the thetan state. Hubbard's system of thought and the practices based on it have been incorporated into a religious body called the Church of Scientology.

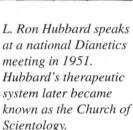

L. Ron Hubbard speaks at a national Dianetics meeting in 1951. Hubbard's therapeutic system later became known as the Church of Scientology.

Activities in therapy groups usually include group training sessions and workshops, but the main interactions occur between the individual member offering therapy and the one receiving it. Therapy groups are often organized like businesses since members must purchase the materials and services provided by the group. Often leadership is in the hands of a committee or small elite group that sets standards and develops and markets the materials and services of the group.

Businesses and structure

It is not unusual for large groups to own and operate businesses or institutions that further their cause or help to support their activities. The Unification Church owns several businesses, has a seminary in New York state, and publishes magazines and newspapers from offices in Washington, D.C. The Hare Krishnas have several farms and a number of restaurants. The Church Universal and

Triumphant maintains a university in Montana. Aum Shinrikyo claimed to own businesses in pottery and semiconductor processing when questioned about the chemicals, also necessary for sarin gas, that were found at their site.

Large groups may have formal governing bodies to oversee various parts of the total organization. For example, the Unification Church has a board of church elders who appoint national presidents for each of the countries where the church is active. Each national president then oversees the local groups in that country. While removed from the daily tasks of administering the group, Rev. Moon remains its inspirational leader.

Some groups have ideas and practices that do not lend themselves to hierarchical or authoritarian structures. This is especially true for magical or occult groups, such as neopagans and witches, who stress the development of each individual's magical powers and personal relationship to the universe, rather than loyalty to a leader.

But most of the groups called cults do have a strong leader, whose personality and ideas have a strong influence on the group's activities. For example, since Rev. Moon seeks to unite all people as one family, the Unification Church emphasizes recruiting many new members to enlarge the cult. Likewise, because Moses David preaches that sexual love shows the love of God, the Family of Love promotes free sexual practices within the cult. And, since Shoko Asahara taught that the world would end in gas attacks that he expected would be directed at him, Aum Shinrikyo cult members manufactured deadly sarin gas and planted it in Tokyo subways, where it killed several people and injured many more.

Unquestioned authority

In most cases the cult leader's wisdom, position, and authority are unquestioned. The leader may be elevated to an exalted or even sacred position, with photographs posted in cult quarters or used as aids in meditation. Followers may try to get as close as they can to the leader, vying for front row seats at lectures. It is reported that Shoko Asahara, who is considered a messiah by his followers, expected cult members to bow and kiss his toe.

Having elevated the leader to such heights, some members report that they find it difficult to think anything he or she does is wrong. Former members of cults with abusive leaders have said that their first impulse was to try to explain the unkind or cruel actions of the leader as lessons for their own good.

Some cult leaders live in luxury, as opposed to the poor lifestyle of their followers. While members may accept luxury as a privilege of the cult leader's position, often they have difficulty understanding a leader's departure from the principles and teachings of the group. Maharaj Ji of the Divine Light Mission, who required his followers to be celibate, lost many members when he himself gave up celibacy to marry his secretary. Similar problems arose among the Branch Davidians when Koresh adopted the practice of taking multiple wives after he had declared that other members should be celibate.

Victims of the nerve gas released on a Tokyo subway await medical attention. Aum Shinrikyo members carried out the lethal assault on the belief that the world would end in gas attacks.

Changes of leadership

Most cults have no formal process for choosing a new leader. When the cult leader dies, or in rare cases is deposed, a new leader must be found. Often a favorite disciple, already active as a secondary leader, moves into the leadership role. Sometimes the wife or adult child of the leader takes over. In either of these cases, the new leader's authority is based on his or her relationship with the previous leader.

If there is conflict over leadership, tensions may escalate until a new leader emerges, unhappy members leave, or the group splits apart. Whatever the reason for a change of leadership, a successful transfer of power is necessary if the cult is to survive.

Dissent

Most cults are rigid, authoritarian structures where there is little room for doubt or dissent. Much dissent is suppressed by members themselves, who quickly learn that questions are not appreciated and that those who are most agreeable to the leader have the most favored treatment or position.

Members who ask questions may be harshly punished, and those who do not want to go along with the program may leave or be asked to leave. One former member of an Eastern-oriented cult recounted that he was asked to leave when he failed to see a bright purple ring around the sun, a phenomenon said to be caused by the group leader and reportedly seen by others in the group. In matters of dissent, the leader or representatives of the leader are the judges. And in the closed system of the cult, there is no appeal beyond the leader.

Cults make their own world

Shut off from the outside world and living in a group that does not tolerate dissent, cult members often live in a world of their own. Those inside the group are "us," and those outside are "them." In this isolated world, the cult leader can be master, as the captain of a ship on the high seas is master of his vessel. A man who knew Shoko Asahara, leader of the Aum Shinrikyo cult, comments that Asahara was attempting to create such a closed world: "He is trying to create a society separate from ordinary society in which he can become king of the castle."[30]

5

Cults and the Outside World

SOME OF THE groups called cults, especially those that are noncommunal, coexist easily with the outside world. Although members may have unorthodox beliefs, their appearance and manner do not make them stand apart from the rest of society. Their meetings and activities do not involve outsiders or impinge upon them, and efforts to recruit are low-key.

Occasionally a particular belief or practice will cause a conflict with mainstream attitudes. For example, Christian Scientists sometimes clash with authorities over the issue of medical care, usually for a child who is being kept from some traditional medical treatment because of the parent's beliefs. However, the issue usually remains limited to the specific incident and does not draw the entire group into tension with the outside world.

Some cults reach out to the community around them in an effort to become known and accepted. Researchers contend that groups with open pathways of communication are better able to accommodate themselves to the world at large. This, in turn, increases the chances that the group will survive and grow.

Some cults emphasize their differences

Some groups choose to emphasize their difference from mainstream society, often by a certain manner of dress or a special hairstyle. For example, neighbors and work associates reported that the members of Heaven's Gate, both male and female, all wore their hair in the same short style, and they also dressed alike. One person reported that they all wore jumpsuits; another saw them all in loose pants and smocklike shirts. Videos showed them all wearing jackets with a "Heaven's Gate" shoulder patch. In like fashion, members of the Manson Family showed their solidarity during the long trial for the Tate murders by shaving their heads and marking their foreheads with an "x" or a swastika when their leader did.

Some groups become highly visible when their members witness for the faith by participating in public demonstrations, such as chanting, handing out literature, or fund-raising. Because they appear different, act in an unusual manner, or try to convince others of their beliefs, cult members may be laughed at, ridiculed, or rejected by noncult members. Facing this hostility from the public underscores for cult members the difference between them and the outside world.

Cults create boundaries

The boundaries that a cult erects may be visible ones. Members may isolate themselves within their living center as the Branch Davidians did at their rural compound outside Waco, Texas. Within its walls, approximately one hun-

Marshall Applewhite addresses his followers in a videotape. Heaven's Gate members' cropped hair and identical clothing affirmed their unity as a group while distinguishing them from the outside world.

Young Manson Family women keep a vigil outside the Los Angeles Hall of Justice to show their support for leader Charles Manson during his trial.

dred people, including a number of families, lived secluded lives. The children had their school lessons within the compound, and some had never been outside its premises. When a number of children were released during the standoff with federal officials in 1993, they told social work personnel that they thought the outside world was a dangerous place. Many groups that withdraw from society share the feeling that the outside world is contaminated and unsafe.

Physical seclusion from society is not the only way a group maintains its boundaries. When members go to jobs or children go to public schools, they often find that their attitudes and values separate them from coworkers or fellow students in the outside world. And cult members seldom socialize outside the group, keeping interactions to a minimum. For example, while the business contacts of Heaven's Gate members found them pleasant and talented in the work setting, neighbors at their rented mansion commented that group members shunned social contacts and disappeared indoors when they waved or attempted to greet them.

The heavy demands cults make on their members' time also serve as effective boundaries. When cult duties interfere with family or other relationships, the cult member becomes increasingly isolated within the group.

Conflicts with families of members

The tendency of cults to isolate members from their families can set the stage for bitter conflicts. Such conflicts played a part in the cult controversy that grew in the 1960s and 1970s. Many of the new cults that formed at that time attracted young adults, whose parents were often unhappy with their child's decision to enter a cult or new religion.

Some parents were distressed that their children had left the religion in which they had been raised. Many saw the end of their hopes and plans for their child's future when he or she gave up education or employment to enter the cult. Parents did not understand the changes in their children's behavior, especially if they adopted special dress or eating habits, practiced meditation, or recited religious mantras or phrases. They were particularly troubled if they thought the living conditions of the group were unhealthy, or if they worried that their child was being exploited for the group's purposes.

Parents who went to cult communes in search of their children sometimes found that they were not permitted to see them, or that they could be with them only in the com-

Parents may be upset by the new habits of a child who has joined a cult, including wearing different clothing and reciting religious phrases. Here, robe-clad Hare Krishna members dance and chant.

pany of another cult member. Some cults had a policy of limiting the new member's outside contacts as part of the process of drawing them into the group. Others wanted to help their new members resist parental pressure to leave the group.

As a result, many parents feared that their children were being held against their will. When cult members came home to visit, some parents tried to convince them not to return to the group. Some sought the help of deprogrammers in an attempt to break their child's attachment to the group.

While conflicts with families surface most often when the cult member is a child or young adult, they also occur when an elderly person joins a cult. In short, any individual who is considered to need the advice and help of family members in making decisions can trigger this conflict.

Organized efforts to control cults

The first organized efforts to control cults came from parents whose children had joined the Children of God. The Parents Committee to Free Our Children from the Children of God, popularly called FREECOG, was formed in the early 1970s. Believing that their children had been programmed to accept the group's beliefs by drugs, hypnosis, or brainwashing techniques, many parents looked to deprogramming as a way to remove their children from the group's influence.

Ted Patrick Jr., one of the founders of FREECOG, introduced the first efforts at deprogramming—a coercive technique to break the cult member's ties to the group. Because deprogramming involves the forcible restraint of the person being deprogrammed, it was quickly attacked by some of the cult members subjected to it, as well as by the cults themselves and groups concerned with civil and religious freedom. While some anticultists continue to recommend forcible techniques, most now encourage "exit counseling," a procedure in which the cult member agrees to meet with deprogrammers, counselors, and family to discuss and reconsider his or her choice.

An aerial view shows the aftermath of the mass suicides and murders at Jonestown. The incident shocked the public and started a wave of anticult sentiment.

By 1974 a national anticult organization called the Citizen's Freedom Foundation had been formed. In 1976 this group, later called Cult Awareness Network (CAN), along with other smaller anticult groups, persuaded Senator Robert Dole of Kansas to hold hearings in Washington, D.C., on the subject of cults. Of particular concern to parents at the time was Rev. Moon's Unification Church. No action resulted from the Dole hearings, but the anticult groups continued to publish national newsletters, give public programs on the dangers of cults, and help families contact deprogrammers.

In 1978 public concern was again aroused when the People's Temple ended in violence at Jonestown. Besides the 912 cult members who died, Congressman Leo Ryan and four aides who had arrived to investigate charges against the group were ambushed and killed by Jones's security personnel. Prompted by these events, anticultists formed the American Family Foundation, a research and educational organization founded "to assist cult victims and their families through the study of cultic groups and manipulative techniques of persuasion and control."[31] Together with the Cult Awareness Network, the American Family Foundation has been the primary representative of the anticult forces.

According to Melton, efforts by the anticult movement to pass laws against cults, or to introduce laws that favor the actions of anticultists, have been unsuccessful. Many people believe such laws would violate the constitutional guarantees of religious freedom. Melton cites as an example the effort of anticultists in 1988 to lobby congressional leaders to pass a bill making the tenth anniversary of the Jonestown tragedy the occasion for a national anticult awareness week. According to Melton, "The bill was gaining support until legislators who were members of several groups which had been targeted as 'cults' over the years (primarily Mormons) killed the bill and substituted a religious freedom celebration in its stead."[32]

Christian anticult measures

Some groups among the Protestant Christian churches, which make up the religious mainstream in the United States, have also been involved in anticult activities. Considering unorthodox beliefs false, heretical, or against orthodox teaching, representatives of these traditional religious groups had been warning against cults and their heresies since the early 1900s. By the mid-1960s, Asian religions entering the United States attracted their attention, as did some early cults, such as Children of God and the People's Temple, which were led by Christian ministers or grew out of Christian initiatives.

Representatives of orthodox Christian faiths have joined parents in efforts to steer young adults and others away from joining cults or alternative religions. According to Melton, over five

The Children of God member in the foreground of this 1969 photo holds a sign warning of the destruction his cult believed was looming in the near future.

hundred Christian countercult ministries existed by the 1980s. At the present time, he states, countercult ministries focus mostly on the New Age movement. This is a collection of widely divergent groups that incorporate ideas from the occult traditions and Eastern religions into Western spirituality. New Age beliefs, such as the belief in reincarnation, conflict with orthodox Christian beliefs and draw members away from traditional faiths.

Lawsuits

Both sides of the cult controversy have used, or tried to use, the courts to mediate their conflicts. Parents have asked courts to grant conservatorship of their adult children to them on the basis that cult membership indicated mental incompetence. This status would give parents the legal right to make decisions for their children so they could legally remove them from the cult. However, most requests for conservatorship, which was meant primarily to protect the elderly or incapacitated, have not been granted.

Melton finds that the anticult movement has had little success in its civil court suits. Even when a lower court delivered a judgment in favor of the anticult group or individual, he notes that the judgment was usually reversed on appeal. For example, a lower court award of $2 million to a former member who sued the Church of Scientology was not upheld on appeal to a higher court.

Cults and cult members have also used the courts to answer their critics. Some members who had been kidnapped from their cult and subjected to deprogramming techniques have successfully sued their deprogrammers and received cash settlements. In the mid-1980s a group known as the Local Church brought a successful libel suit against the Christian anticult ministry called the Spiritual Counterfeits Project (SCP). Claiming that allegations published by SCP against it were malicious and false, the Local Church won a judgment of $11 million. This large award caused the SCP to declare bankruptcy. Another anticult group, CAN, was similarly forced into bankruptcy in 1996, after losing a series of lawsuits with members of the Church of Scientology.

Confrontations and response

The charges leveled against cults have sometimes led to official investigations and confrontations with authorities. Among the earliest were charges of polygamy and sexual manipulation against the Children of God and its leader. As a result of investigations in California and New York, this group has largely disappeared from the United States and now exists primarily in other countries. According to Melton,

> The sexual manipulation in the Children of God has now been so thoroughly documented that it is doubtful whether the organization can ever, in spite of whatever future reforms it might initiate, regain any respectable place in the larger religious community.[33]

While outlawed in Spain, it continues to recruit in other countries and was reported to be active in the eastern European nation of Bulgaria as recently as the early 1990s.

It was in response to charges that members of the People's Temple were being forced to live in unsanitary and substandard conditions that Congressman Ryan arrived in Jonestown to investigate. Under the threat of this official scrutiny, Jones and other cult leaders resorted to the violence that left almost 1,000 people dead.

Charges of possession of illegal firearms and child abuse featured prominently in the confrontation that brought about the destruction of the Branch Davidians of Waco. Child abuse charges had been filed, investigated, and dropped in 1992, but confrontation escalated over the firearms charges. The vigor and force with which federal officials pursued these charges were met by equally strong resistance and violence from Koresh and his followers. Both federal agents and cult members were killed in the initial clash that preceded a seven-week-long standoff. During that time, the child abuse concerns resurfaced as part of the rationale for the extreme force used by federal officials against Koresh and the group. In the final conflagration, seventy-four Branch Davidians died, twenty-one of them children.

Public perception

Mass murders and suicides, armed standoffs, and fiery destructions are newsworthy items that attract the public's attention and shape its perception about groups labeled "cults." A second major influence on public perception is the information offered by so-called cult experts who oppose cults for personal or religious reasons.

Academic researchers point out that many of the cult experts who are quoted in the media are not researchers who study alternative religious groups; instead, they are members of the anticult movement or deprogrammers, many of whom do not have credentials as mental health counselors. These sources, researchers claim, give a one-sided perspective on a group. According to James Lewis, a scholar of new religious movements,

> It is, in fact, the two-decade-long interaction between the anticult movement and the media that has been largely responsible for the widespread view that all new or unconventional religions, that is "cults," are dangerous organizations—this in

spite of the fact that comparatively few such groups constitute a general threat, either to themselves or to society.[34]

The stereotype of cults promotes the idea that cults are all alike, that they use mind control to entrap and control members, and that leaders are evil manipulators who exploit their helpless followers for their own gain. The highly negative publicity that many recent groups have received reinforces such stereotypes. Researchers Anson D. Shupe Jr. and Jeffrey K. Hadden say that "the mere labeling of a group as a cult conjures up the most scandalous of images."[35]

Religious scholars and academics are not the only ones who have begun to avoid the term "cult" because of its negative connotations. In Australia, the term was banned from proceedings in a recent court case against the Family of Love because the court deemed it to be prejudicial.

The ruins of the Branch Davidian compound in Waco, Texas, are a bleak testament to the deaths that occurred in the 1993 confrontation between members and federal agents.

Three members of a Satanic group. Some Satanists participate in criminal activities meant to defile Christian traditions.

Some cults advocate violence

Some cults foster antisocial ideas and direct hostility and violence toward the outside world. Aum Shinrikyo, with its poison gas attacks, is a recent example. In addition to the attacks carried out in Japan, there is some evidence, according to testimony given in court, that attacks were also planned for other countries.

Small groups of Satanists also engage in antisocial and illegal activities. Usually these are informal groups who direct their hostility against Christian religious practices. These groups leave Satanic symbols and ritual materials or animal mutilations at the site of their vandalism or crime. Satanist groups, like other groups that commit illegal acts, keep themselves secret to avoid detection. Typically, they remain unknown to the general public until some newsworthy event occurs.

Members may leave at a point of crisis

When a cult comes into extreme conflict with the outside world, or reaches a point of internal crisis, growing tensions may cause some members to leave. Some Branch Davidians left their compound when given the opportunity during the siege by federal officials. Survivors of the People's Temple fled into the jungle of Guyana rather than follow their leader to death. A surviving member of Heaven's Gate left the group only a month before its mass suicide, saying he had developed a disturbing feeling as the critical moment approached. While some cult members remain committed to the death, moments of crisis propel others into the outside world.

6

Leaving a Cult

RESEARCHERS FIND THAT cults, or alternative religions, have a high turnover in membership. While most who leave a cult do so within the first year or two, some may stay many years before deciding to leave. Margaret Thaler Singer tells of counseling people coming out of cults after twenty-five or more years of membership.

Some become disillusioned

Some members leave when they find that the cult or its leader does not live up to their expectations or the ideal of perfection that the group claimed. Idealistic members of groups like the Divine Light Mission, which claimed to "save the world," often became disillusioned when they saw that the world was not changing as a result of their efforts.

Many members of the Unification Church became disillusioned when they were encouraged to use deceitful practices in recruiting new members and during fund-raising. One member wondered if he himself had been recruited by this "heavenly deception." He had worked enthusiastically for the cause as a writer for one of its newsletters, but he quickly became disenchanted when he was instructed to solicit money on the street, claiming that the donations were for a children's home that he knew did not exist. While many cult members could justify these unethical practices because of their belief in the cause, others found that the deception conflicted with their moral code and the ideals that had inspired them to join the group.

One woman reported leaving Children of God when Moses David encouraged prostitution as a way to recruit new members. A number of Branch Davidians left the group when Koresh took multiple wives, especially one who was under the legal age of marriage. Another couple left the People's Temple when they could no longer bear to see the cruel humiliations and severe physical punishments meted out to members by Rev. Jim Jones.

Some members become discouraged about their own place or personal prospects within the group. For example, a woman in the Unification Church waited six years to be "blessed," that is, matched in marriage with another member, an event for which members became eligible after three years. Finally, despairing of reaching this personal goal, she left the group.

Another former member recounts that hardworking members of his Unification Church commune became resentful when they did not receive credit for their outstanding fund-raising efforts, which included setting up a small yet highly successful candle-making business. Credit was given instead to regional group leaders, who had not been directly involved in the work. Later, this entire commune, with the exception of one member, left the Unification Church.

Attitudes may change

Sometimes members find that their attitudes change over time, prompting them to leave the group. Many people join at young ages and as they mature, they tire of the regimen or restrictions of the cult and the self-sacrifice expected of them.

One man reported leaving the Hare Krishnas because he felt his life in the group was too limited. For example, he had tired of the celibate life and wanted a mature sexual relationship. As a member of the group, however, he was not permitted to make this choice. At last, the restrictions on his ability to make free choices led him away from the group. As he told authors Stoner and Parke, "I began to want very strongly to be free, on my own, and living exactly as I felt was right." [36] Although he chose to leave the

Hare Krishnas in Boston celebrate the reversal of a $1.3 million judgment against their group. The suit was brought about by a former Hare Krishna member who charged the group with causing emotional distress.

group, he still believes his experience with the Krishnas was valuable in his development as a person.

The process of attitude change is often subtle, proceeding step-by-step until finally the member realizes that he or she no longer feels committed. This gradual disengagement was described by one member who left the Unification Church. He found himself going to see his parents, who lived nearby, more frequently. Then he and two other members used the cult car to take a week-long, unauthorized driving trip. It was not until they were on the return trip, he said, that he realized he would not remain in the group.

Attachments to family

Some members leave groups when they feel membership threatens their relationships with family or loved ones. Young people may miss their contacts with parents and friends over time and choose to return to the outside world and these important emotional connections. Mothers of young children have reported leaving a group because the cult wanted too much of their time, keeping them away from their children. Others rebelled at the group's requirement that babies and young children be tended by communal day care, designed to strengthen the connection of child to group at the expense of the bond between parent and child.

Married couples have left groups in order to reduce stress on their marriage. They comment that it was difficult to develop their relationship when work assignments separated them, the cult demanded excessive amounts of their time and energy, or the group exerted pressure on one spouse to affect the behavior of the other. Deciding that their marriage was more of a priority than the group, they left.

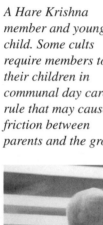

A Hare Krishna member and young child. Some cults require members to put their children in communal day care, a rule that may cause friction between parents and the group.

Difficulties of leaving the group

Even when cult members are inclined to leave the group, there are strong forces that hold them back. The first step in leaving requires the cult member to admit it was a mistake to join. Many find it hard to admit having made a mistake, especially if family and friends are critical of the group and unsupportive of the member's participation. Another obstacle to leaving is the necessity to give up friends in the group. For many cult members, other members are the only social contacts they have. They know that these friendships will have to be given up and leaving them may be a deep personal loss. The task is made more difficult when friends try to convince the member to stay or instill doubt as to whether the member will be welcomed home again by parents and family.

Sometimes cult members must also leave behind a spouse or child. This can happen because they act alone for fear of disapproval or pressures from other members to stay, or it can happen because other family members may not want to leave. When Jeannie Mills and her husband left the People's Temple, which was located in San Francisco at the time, their teenage daughter elected to remain. Mills recalls, "Our oldest daughter, Linda, had decided that she wasn't ready to leave the church, so she moved into the temple commune." [37]

Fears about leaving

Members of groups who believe the outside world is impure and that salvation lies with the group must face fears for their spiritual welfare as well as distrust of society in order to leave. This is a special problem for young people who have been born, raised, and educated in a cult and know little of the outside world.

Besides the uncertainties of life outside the cult, members often fear reprisals or revenge by the group for leaving. In extreme cases, people who want to leave have been told that they would be hunted down or that they and their families would be injured or killed if they left. When the Mills family left the People's Temple, they planned their escape carefully, fearing that they would not be allowed to go if the leadership knew; others who had left the group had been attacked and severely beaten.

Fears of retaliation are especially likely to be felt by members leaving groups that indulge in illegal activities, have authoritarian and punitive leaders, or have a tendency to violence. Even though the feared retribution may not occur, especially since most groups are more interested in recruiting new members than harassing former ones, a cult member who decides to leave must face the anxiety such fears produce.

What is the alternative?

The crucial question for a member leaving a communal cult is where to go or what to do next. Former members often have no friends in the outside world, especially if they have been in the cult for many years. They may doubt that old friends will accept them and fear that parents will not be receptive to them, particularly if they harshly cut off contact with their parents when they entered the cult.

Members who want to leave a cult may have no money to do so, having given all they had or all they earned to the group. Those who entered at an early age may have no advanced education or job skills, and no employment history to help them get a job. Members who left college educations or promising jobs may find it difficult to take up where they left off. Also, the need to find new motivations and a new direction in life can appear an insurmountable problem.

A former member of the Unification Church mused on the problem of entering "cult member" on a job résumé and wondered what kind of employment six years of following a cult leader could prepare one for. He also spoke of a friend who had been demoted from a leadership position in the group and required to go back to an intense one-hundred-day basic training session. When he asked himself why his friend did not leave, he realized that "perhaps he felt he had no alternative."[38]

The lack of an alternative plan, or just not knowing how to go about creating a life on one's own, keeps some members in cults who might otherwise leave and causes some who do leave to return. It was in part the desire of parents or other relatives to help cult members see alternatives to cult life that led to the controversial practice known as deprogramming.

Deprogramming

When Ted Patrick Jr. pioneered the use of deprogramming in the early 1970s, many families looked to this procedure for help in removing their loved one from a cult. Deprogramming is based on the belief that cults brainwash members or control their thinking, taking away the free will of members so they will accept the cult leader's beliefs and instructions.

The term "brainwash" is based on a Chinese phrase used to describe the process Chinese Communists used to change the attitudes of prisoners of war in the 1950s. This process consisted of prolonged interrogations and other abusive psychological techniques prisoners were forced to endure. As critics of the idea that cults use brainwashing point out, a crucial component of the process is physical restraint, or coercion, a factor usually missing from the cult experience.

Families in the 1970s began to forcibly remove loved ones from cults, such as this Indian-based religion, and subject them to deprogramming.

Believing that cults programmed their members to accept the cult message, Ted Patrick and others used similar psychological techniques, in a coercive setting, to deprogram cult members and restore their previous attitudes.

Before cult members could be deprogrammed, however, they had to be removed from the group. To do this, some parents sought the help of the courts and asked to be granted conservatorship of the cult member. If granted, conservatorship generally lasted for a limited time, perhaps weeks or months, during which time the family could legally remove the cult member and subject

them to deprogramming. Some courts granted conservatorship, but many would not.

In many cases, parents forcibly detained their children or tricked them into a meeting with deprogrammers. Some parents even hired people to kidnap their children at some opportune moment when they were off cult premises so they could be deprogrammed.

Deprogramming involves long sessions of interrogation and badgering by the deprogrammer and associates, who are often former cult members. They criticize the cult and the cult leader and relate stories of other members who have left. They might berate the cult member for choosing to be in the group and shame them for causing pain to their family. Often family members are present to urge the cult member to leave and to make assurances of help and support.

Typically, several deprogrammers or helpers take turns bombarding the member with statements, keeping him or her awake for long hours. Often the deprogramming takes place in a locked room, secured against escape. The cult member is given no privacy, sometimes even being accom-

panied to the bathroom. Some people who have undergone the process report being told that they would not be released until they agreed to leave the cult. Deprogamming usually lasts for two or three days in an unremitting attack on the cult's beliefs and the member's decision to be in the group.

Pros and cons of deprogramming

Some members have been convinced to leave their groups through deprogramming. Many of them adopted the ideas of their deprogrammers and became active in movements to get other people out of cults. Some became deprogrammers themselves. Researchers who oppose the method have raised the question of whether successful deprogramming truly allows the cult member to exercise free choice or whether it simply converts the member to the anticult group by the same techniques they accuse cults of using.

Some people who have left cults after deprogramming have expressed their gratitude for the family intervention that helped them overcome resistance to leaving or helped them see an alternative to cult life.

Some pointed out that deprogramming helped them break bonds of friendship with other cult members, making it easier to leave the group.

Other members who were deprogrammed returned to their groups. Some, seeing that escape was impossible, pretended to be convinced by deprogrammers until they were released and then secretly made plans to return. A failed deprogramming usually widened the gap between the cult member and family who initiated the procedure, and a returned cult member often disappeared more deeply into the cult. Sometimes he or she was sent to another commune or even a foreign country.

Exit counseling

Families reluctant to use coercive techniques can sometimes convince their loved ones to agree to a kind of negotiated deprogramming. In this process, the member agrees to meet with family and counselors, to listen to information about the cult that they might not know, and to hear criticisms of the leader, beliefs, and practices of the group. This voluntary meeting, away from the pressure of other cult members, is designed to give the individual an opportunity to reevaluate his or her membership. The cult member then decides whether to leave the cult or to return. This practice is now called exit counseling. According to Margaret Thaler Singer,

> The term *exit counseling* first came into use to distinguish voluntary interventions from deprogrammings. Today, exit counseling identifies the educational process that takes place in efforts to get cult members to reevaluate their membership. In fact, "deprogramming" is in many ways a more accurate description of the process of getting the cult member to recognize what has happened to him or her, but since that word is now tinged with memories of the early snatchings and restraint, most people are reluctant to use it.[39]

Critics of deprogramming and exit counseling say these procedures employ the same manipulative techniques that cults are accused of using. Proponents say the events simply give members a chance to reconsider their membership free of cult pressures.

Life after cult membership

Former cult members adapt to the outside world with varying degrees of ease or difficulty. While some find their own way with the help of family and friends, others seek therapy with a mental health counselor to help them with problems.

Among the problems former members commonly face, according to Singer, are feelings of low self-esteem, fear of getting involved or making commitments, and reluctance to trust their own instincts. She identifies these symptoms as those of delayed stress syndrome, caused by cult membership or the effects of thought reform.

Other researchers, however, dispute Singer's interpretation. While Melton acknowledges that some former cult members have left groups because they suffered psychological or physical abuse, he maintains that those who have been deprogrammed have also left their cult under stressful conditions. He refers to recent studies indicating that primarily the cult members who leave as a result of deprogramming, and not those who leave voluntarily, show symptoms of delayed stress syndrome. "The great majority of people who leave simply because the group no longer meets their needs," asserts Melton, "show no pattern of psychological disturbance." [40]

Whatever the reason for leaving the cult, and no matter whether a cult member is deprogrammed or leaves voluntarily, he or she faces the challenge of finding a new place in the world. No longer relying on the group to provide personal relationships, former cult members must find new social contacts or renew old ones. If the cult furnished a place to live, they must find new homes and means of financial support. Above all, without the group's goals, they must find new direction and perhaps new values to guide them.

Notes

Chapter 1: Definition and History

1. J. Gordon Melton, *The Encyclopedic Handbook of Cults in America.* New York: Garland Publishing, 1992, p. 7.
2. Margaret Thaler Singer with Janja Lalich, *Cults in Our Midst.* San Francisco: Jossey-Bass Publishers, 1995, p. xx.
3. David G. Bromley and Anson D. Shupe Jr., *Strange Gods: The Great American Cult Scare.* Boston: Beacon Press, 1981, p. 4.
4. Elizabeth C. Nordbeck, "The Great American Cult Controversy," *USA Today*, vol. 121, no. 2568, September 1992, p. 79.
5. Nordbeck, "The Great American Cult Controversy," p. 79.
6. Quoted in Terry Wilson, "Out of Public Eye, but Keeping Faith," *Chicago Tribune*, January 24, 1997, sec. 2, p. 7.
7. Melton, *The Encyclopedic Handbook*, p. 109.
8. Jeffrey S. Victor, "Satanic Cults' Ritual Abuse of Children: Horror or Hoax?" *USA Today*, vol. 122, no. 2582, November 1993, p. 60.
9. Quoted in Bromley and Shupe, *Strange Gods*, p. xii.
10. Melton, *The Encyclopedic Handbook*, p. 7.

Chapter 2: Joining a Cult

11. Quoted in Bromley and Shupe, *Strange Gods*, p. 179.
12. Quoted in Marc Galanter, *Cults: Faith, Healing, and Coercion.* New York: Oxford University Press, 1989, p. 54.
13. Singer, *Cults in Our Midst*, p. 20.
14. Quoted in Allen Tate Wood, *Moonstruck.* New York: William Morrow, 1979, p. 76.
15. Singer, *Cults in Our Midst*, p. 120.

16. Melton, *The Encyclopedic Handbook*, p. 15.
17. Singer, *Cults in Our Midst*, p. 25.
18. Melton, *The Encyclopedic Handbook*, p. 8.

Chapter 3: Life in a Cult

19. Quoted in Arthur J. Deikman, *The Wrong Way Home: Uncovering the Patterns of Cult Behavior in American Society*. Boston: Beacon Press, 1994, p. 11.
20. Vincent Bugliosi, *Helter Skelter*. New York: W. W. Norton, 1974, p. 233.
21. Carroll Stoner and Jo Anne Parke, *All God's Children*. New York: Penguin Books, 1977, pp. 191–92.
22. Stoner and Parke, *All God's Children*, p. 192.
23. Francine Jeanne Daner, *The American Children of Krsna: A Study of the Hare Krsna Movement*. New York: Holt, Rinehart & Winston, 1976, p. 68.
24. Quoted in Bugliosi, *Helter Skelter*, p. 225.
25. Robert Balch, "Looking Behind the Scenes in a Religious Cult: Implications for the Study of Conversion," *Sociological Analysis*, Summer 1980, p. 142.

Chapter 4: Cult Organization

26. William S. Bainbridge and Rodney Stark, "Cult Formation: Three Compatible Models," *Sociological Analysis*, Winter 1979, p. 283.
27. Quoted in Bugliosi, *Helter Skelter*, p. 484.
28. Scott Lowe, "The Strange Case of Franklin Jones," in David Christopher Lane, *Exposing Cults: When the Skeptical Mind Confronts the Mystical*. New York: Garland Publishing, 1994, p. 75.
29. Quoted in Wood, *Moonstruck*, p. 149.
30. Quoted in James Walsh, "Shoko Asahara: The Making of a Messiah," *Time*, April 3, 1995, p. 31.

Chapter 5: Cults and the Outside World

31. Marcia R. Rudin, ed., *Cults on Campus: Continuing Challenge*. New York: American Family Foundation, 1991.

32. Melton, *The Encyclopedic Handbook*, p. 350.

33. Melton, *The Encyclopedic Handbook*, p. 230.

34. James R. Lewis, "Self-Fulfilling Stereotypes, the Anti-cult Movement, and the Waco Confrontation," in Stuart A. Wright, ed., *Armageddon in Waco: Critical Perspectives on the Branch Davidian Conflict*. Chicago: University of Chicago Press, 1995, pp. 97–98.

35. Anson Shupe and Jeffrey K. Hadden, "Cops, News Copy, and Public Opinion," in Wright, *Armageddon in Waco*, p. 180.

Chapter 6: Leaving a Cult

36. Quoted in Stoner and Parke, *All God's Children*, p. 419.

37. Jeannie Mills, *Six Years with God: Life Inside Reverend Jim Jones's Peoples Temple*, New York: A & W Publishers, 1979, p. 314.

38. Quoted in Wood, *Moonstruck*, p. 148.

39. Singer, *Cults in Our Midst*, p. 286.

40. Melton, *The Encyclopedic Handbook*, p. 19.

Glossary

brainwashing: Application, by force, of intense and prolonged techniques of psychological persuasion, designed to indoctrinate a person to a certain belief system.

celibate: Unmarried or abstaining from sexual relations, especially for religious reasons.

charismatic: Having to do with charisma, the magnetic power of a leader to attract and hold followers.

coercive: Serving or intended to control by force, threat, or other pressure.

commune: A group practicing communal living.

conservatorship: Legal status by which a person takes over and manages the interests of an adult who is considered incompetent to make decisions in his or her own best interest.

conversion: Change from one religion or belief system to another.

delayed stress syndrome: A collection of psychological symptoms, including depression and low self-confidence, that show up in a person after he or she has endured a stressful situation or problem and are attributed to that stress.

deprogrammer: One who works to change the attitudes and thinking of a person believed to be the victim of brainwashing, mind control, or thought reform.

disaffected: Discontented or estranged.

disciple: Follower, especially one who follows the religious doctrines of another.

exit counseling: A process of education and persuasion, without the use of force, by which deprogrammers, counselors, and parents attempt to convince cult members to leave their chosen group.

fundamentalist: One who believes in the literal and absolute truth of religious scriptures, for example, the Bible for Christians or the Koran for Muslims.

guru: Personal spiritual teacher in Hinduism.

heavenly deception: Phrase referring to a religious group's dishonest practices in recruitment or fund-raising.

heretical: Having to do with beliefs different from the accepted doctrines of a religion.

Koran: Sacred scriptures of Islam.

mantra: Words, or prayers, used as a ritual devotion in Hinduism and Buddhism, such as the Hare Krishna chant.

meditation: Spiritual exercise, using special breathing, chanting, or other techniques to achieve a higher state of consciousness.

messiah: An expected deliverer, or savior, of a religious group.

mind control: Popular term to indicate psychological techniques used to influence and control others, especially in a harmful way.

monastic: Having to do with monks or other persons living in seclusion from the world as part of a religious group.

New Age movement: A variety of groups whose ideas combine beliefs from Eastern religions and the occult, such as reincarnation, with doctrines of Western religions.

occult: Beyond the bounds of ordinary knowledge, such as magic.

patriarch: The male head of a family or tribe, especially those of the biblical Israelites.

pejorative: Having a disparaging or belittling force.

polemicists: Those engaging in argument or controversy.

polygamy: The practice of having more than one spouse, particularly wives.

reincarnation: The belief that the soul moves to another body or form after death.

sankirtana: The practice of chanting in public by Krishna devotees.

socialization: Process of education or training by which a person learns the beliefs and habits of the society or group of which he or she is a member.

stereotype: A set idea, oversimplified opinion, or unthinking judgment applied to a person, group, or issue.

swami: A term of respectful address to a Hindu spiritual leader or religious teacher.

Theosophist: One who follows Theosophy, the name given to various forms of religious belief based on a combination of Eastern ideas and the occult.

thetans: Term for the celestial beings that are the souls, or essences, of people, according to L. Ron Hubbard, founder of the Church of Scientology.

thought reform: Term referring to the process of manipulating psychological and social factors to change people's attitudes and behavior; also called brainwashing or mind control.

unorthodox: Not following the accepted beliefs or doctrines, especially of a religion.

witnessing: Giving public testimony of one's religious faith.

yogi: A Hindu spiritual teacher or leader.

Organizations
to Contact

The following organizations provide information or services relating to cults and cult membership. Their addresses and phone numbers are provided so each organization can be contacted directly.

American Family Foundation (AFF)
PO Box 2265
Bonita Springs, FL 34133
(212) 533-5420

The AFF is a research and educational organization founded to "assist cult victims and their families through the study of cultic groups and manipulative techniques of persuasion and control." The foundation publishes books and other educational materials, conducts conferences, and lists anticult resources throughout the world.

Cult Awareness Network (CAN)
1680 N. Vine St., Suite 415
Los Angeles, CA 90028
(800) 556-3055
Internet: http://www.cultawarenessnetwork.org

Recently reorganized with the stated goal of promoting religious tolerance, CAN maintains information about religious groups, publishes educational brochures and booklets, sponsors conferences open to the public, and gives referrals to qualified experts.

Holy Spirit Association for the Unification of World Christianity (Unification Church)
4 W. 43rd St.
New York, NY 10036
(212) 997-0050
Internet: http://www.unification.org/index.html

The Unification Church maintains a network of centers throughout the world, including its national headquarters in New York City.

International Cult Education Program (ICEP)
PO Box 2265
Bonita Springs, FL 34133
(212) 533-5420

The ICEP, affiliated with the American Family Foundation, helps leaders in schools, churches, and other groups educate themselves and their group members about cults. It provides speakers and educational materials designed to warn the public about the dangers of pyschological manipulation and the cults that practice it.

International Society for Krishna Consciousness (ISKCON)
ISKCON of Illinois
1716 W. Lunt Ave.
Chicago, IL 60626
(773) 973-0900
Internet: http://www.webcom.com/ara/col/others/

In addition to its Chicago temple, ISKCON maintains temples in many cities throughout the world. All provide information about Krishna to interested inquirers. For a list of centers throughout the world, computer users can contact the Hare Krishna website.

Suggestions for Further Reading

Willa Appel, *Cults in America: Programmed for Paradise*. New York: Holt, Rinehart & Winston, 1983.

Daniel Cohen, *Cults*. Brookfield, CT: Millbrook Press, 1994.

John J. Collins, *Cult Experience: An Overview of Cults, Their Traditions, and Why People Join Them*. Springfield, IL: C. C. Thomas, 1991.

Susan Meredith, *Usborne Book of World Religion*. London: Usborne Publishing, 1995.

Kay M. Porterfield, *Straight Talk about Cults*. New York: Facts On File, 1995.

Thomas Streissguth, *Charismatic Cult Leaders*. Minneapolis: Oliver Press, 1995.

Works Consulted

William S. Bainbridge and Rodney Stark, "Cult Formation: Three Compatible Models," *Sociological Analysis*, Winter 1979.

——, "Scientology: To Be Perfectly Clear," *Sociological Analysis*, Summer 1980.

Robert Balch, "Looking Behind the Scenes in a Religious Cult: Implications for the Study of Conversion," *Sociological Analysis*, Summer 1980.

Eileen Barker, *The Making of a Moonie: Choice or Brainwashing?* Oxford: Basil Blackwell, 1984.

Fred Bayles and Patrick O'Driscoll, "Cybercults Earn Money, Recruit on Web," *USA Today*, March 28–30, 1997.

James A. Beckford, *Cult Controversies*. London: Tavistock Publications, 1985.

David G. Bromley and Phillip E. Hammond, *The Future of New Religious Movements*. Macon, GA: Mercer University Press, 1987.

David G. Bromley and Anson D. Shupe Jr., *Strange Gods: The Great American Cult Scare*. Boston: Beacon Press, 1981.

Vincent Bugliosi, *Helter Skelter*. New York: W. W. Norton, 1974.

Ian Buruma, "Lost Without a Faith," *Time*, April 3, 1995.

Committee on Psychiatry and Religion, Group for the Advancement of Psychiatry, Report No. 132, *Leaders and Followers: A Psychiatric Perspective on Religious Cults*. Washington, DC: American Psychiatric Press, 1992.

"Court Considers Animal Sacrifice, Airport Witnessing," *Christianity Today*, April 27, 1992.

Francine Jeanne Daner, *The American Children of Krsna: A Study of the Hare Krsna Movement*. New York: Holt, Rinehart & Winston, 1976.

Arthur J. Deikman, *The Wrong Way Home: Uncovering the Patterns of Cult Behavior in American Society*. Boston: Beacon Press, 1994.

Irvin Doress and Jack Nusan Porter, "Kids in Cults," *Society*, May/June 1978.

Robert S. Ellwood Jr., *Alternative Altars: Unconventional and Eastern Spirituality in America*. Chicago: University of Chicago Press, 1979.

Joseph H. Fichter, ed., *Alternatives to American Mainline Churches*. Barrytown, NY: Unification Theological Seminary, 1983.

Marc Galanter, *Cults: Faith, Healing, and Coercion*. New York: Oxford University Press, 1989.

Migene Gonzalez-Wippler, *Santeria: The Religion*. New York: Harmony Books, 1989.

Natalie Isser and Lita Linzer Schwartz, *The History of Conversion and Contemporary Cults*. New York: Peter Lang, 1988.

Roger Kahle, "Keeping Clear of Cults," *Lutheran*, August 1996.

Steve Kloehn, "Most Alternative Sects Are Safe, Experts Say," *Chicago Tribune*, March 28, 1997.

David Christopher Lane, *Exposing Cults: When the Skeptical Mind Confronts the Mystical*. New York: Garland Publishing, 1994.

James R. Lewis, ed., *From the Ashes: Making Sense of Waco*. Lanham, MD: Rowman and Littlefield Publishers, 1994.

Una McManus and John C. Cooper, *Dealing with Destructive Cults*. Grand Rapids, MI: Zondervan Books, 1984.

Flynn McRoberts, "Cult Well-Liked in New Mexico," *Chicago Tribune*, March 30, 1997.

J. Gordon Melton, *The Encyclopedia of American Religions*, 3rd ed. supplement. Detroit: Gale Research, 1992.

———, *The Encyclopedic Handbook of Cults in America*. New York: Garland Publishing, 1992.

J. Gordon Melton and Robert L. Moore, *The Cult Experience: Responding to the New Religious Pluralism*. New York: Pilgrim Press, 1982.

Mark Miller, "Secrets of the Cult," *Newsweek*, April 14, 1997.

Jeannie Mills, *Six Years with God: Life Inside Reverend Jim Jones's Peoples Temple*, New York: A & W Publishers, 1979.

Art Moore, "New Kingdoms for the Cults," *Christianity Today*, January 13, 1992.

Ray Moseley, "In Germany, Scientology Distrusted and Very Unwelcome," *Chicago Tribune*, February 16, 1997.

Elizabeth C. Nordbeck, "The Great American Cult Controversy," *USA Today*, vol. 121, no. 2568, September 1992.

Peter Occhiogrosso, *The Joy of Sects*. New York: Doubleday, 1996.

Loretta Orion, *Never Again the Burning Times: Paganism Revisited*, Prospect Heights, IL: Waveland Press, 1995.

Andrew J. Pavlos, *The Cult Experience*. Westport, CT: Greenwood Press, 1982.

Richard Quebedeaux, ed., *Lifestyle: Conversations with Members of the Unification Church*. New York: Rose of Sharon Press, 1982.

Thomas Robbins, *Cults, Converts and Charisma: The Sociology of New Religious Movements*. London: Sage Publications, 1988.

Marcia R. Rudin, ed., *Cults on Campus: Continuing Challenge*. New York: American Family Foundation, 1991.

Cynthia Stalter Sasse and Peggy Murphy Widder, *The Kirtland Massacre*. New York: Donald I. Fine, 1991.

Vincent J. Schodolski, "Thirty-Nine Men Die in Apparent Mass Suicide," *Chicago Tribune*, March 27, 1997.

Vincent J. Schodolski and Charles M. Madigan, "They Wore Black, Died in Three Waves." *Chicago Tribune*, March 28, 1997.

Bob Secter, "Ideology Merged Science Fiction, Religion," *Chicago Tribune*, March 28, 1997.

Bob Secter and Steve Mills, "Mad Journey Began with One Small Step," *Chicago Tribune*, March 30, 1997.

Anson Shupe and David G. Bromley, eds., *Anti-Cult Movements in Cross-Cultural Perspective*. New York: Garland Publishing, 1994.

Margaret Thaler Singer, "Coming Out of the Cults," *Psychology Today*, January 1979.

Margaret Thaler Singer with Janja Lalich, *Cults in Our Midst*, San Francisco: Jossey-Bass Publishers, 1995.

Carroll Stoner and Jo Anne Parke, *All God's Children*. New York: Penguin Books, 1977.

James D. Tabor and Eugene V. Gallagher, *Why Waco? Cults and the Battle for Religious Freedom in America*. Berkeley: University of California Press, 1995.

David Van Biema, "Prophet of Poison," *Time*, April 3, 1995.

David E. Van Zandt, *Living in the Children of God*. Princeton: Princeton University Press, 1991.

Jeffrey S. Victor, "Satanic Cults' Ritual Abuse of Children: Horror or Hoax?" *USA Today*, vol. 122, no. 2582, November 1993.

Roy Wallis, *Salvation and Protest*. New York: St. Martin's Press, 1979.

James Walsh, "Shoko Asahara: The Making of a Messiah," *Time*, April 3, 1995.

Madhu Bazaz Wangu, *Buddhism: World Religions*. New York: Facts On File, 1993.

——, *Hinduism: World Religions*. New York: Facts On File, 1991.

Thomas W. Wedge with Robert L. Powers, *The Satan Hunter*, Canton, OH: Daring Books, 1987.

Terry Wilson, "Out of Public Eye, but Keeping Faith," *Chicago Tribune*, January 24, 1997.

Allen Tate Wood, *Moonstruck*. New York: William Morrow, 1979.

Stuart A. Wright, ed., *Armageddon in Waco: Critical Perspectives on the Branch Davidian Conflict*. Chicago: University of Chicago Press, 1995.

Jeff Zeleny and Susan Kuczka, "Those Who Said No Shudder with Relief," *Chicago Tribune*, March 30, 1997.

Index

About the Author

Joan D. Barghusen is an educator turned freelance writer. Careers in early childhood education and museum education sharpened her interests in human development and ancient history, including religions of the world. As an educator in an archaeological museum, she wrote many study guides about ancient Egypt, Mesopotamia, and Persia. Her recent publications include an article about the ancient city of Carthage, which she visited three times while working on a project at its archaeological museum.

Picture Credits